Stylistics

SUNY series in Hegelian Studies
William Desmond, editor

Stylistics

Rethinking the Artforms After Hegel

Richard Dien Winfield

State University of New York Press

Published by
State University of New York Press, Albany

For information, address State University of New York Press,
State University Plaza, Albany, NY 12246

Production by Cynthia Tenace Lassonde
Marketing by Dana Yanulavich

Library of Congress Catalog-in-Publication Data

Winfield, Richard Dien, 1950–
Stylistics : rethinking the artforms after Hegel / Richard Dien Winfield.
p. cm. — (SUNY series in Hegelian studies)
Includes bibliographical references and index.
ISBN 0-7914-2781-1 (alk. paper). — ISBN 0-7914-2782-X (pbk. : alk. paper)
1. Aesthetics. 2. Arts. 3. Hegel, Georg Wilhelm Friedrich, 1770-1831—Influence. I. Title. II. Series.
BH39.W556 1996
111'.85—dc20 95-11121
CIP

10 9 8 7 6 5 4 3 2 1

In memory of Isaac Soyer,
painter and teacher.

Contents

Acknowledgments ix
Introduction 1

1. **The Problem of Artistic Style: Conceiving the Particular Forms of Art** 7–26
   Controversies in Moving Beyond the Universal Features of Art 7
   The Artforms as Minimal Particularizations of Art 13
   The Ordering of the Artforms 17
   The Hierarchy of Artforms and the End of Art 19
   The Logical Differentiation of the Forms of Art 21
   The Basic Taxonomy of the Symbolic, Classical, and Romantic Forms of Art 22

2. **The Symbolic Form of Art** 27–50
   Preliminary Difficulties in Characterizing the Symbolic Form of Art 27
   The Role of the Symbol in Symbolic Art 29
   The Content of Symbolic Art 33
      The Construal of the Divine in Symbolic Art 34
      The Construal of Conduct in Symbolic Art 36
   The External Reality, Creation, and Reception of Symbolic Art 37
   The Primacy of Symbolic Art 38
   The Differentiation of Types of Symbolic Art 40
   The Completeness of the Varieties of Symbolic Art 49

3.	**The Classical Form of Art**	51–72
	Preliminary Controversies in Conceiving Classical Art	51
	Is the Symbolic Artform the Historical and Conceptual Prerequisite of Classical Art?	53
	The Meaning and Shape of the Classical Form	57
	Hegel's Suspect Limitations upon the Classical Form	59
	The Classical Construal of the Divine and Conduct	63
	The External Reality, Creation, and Reception of Classical Art	65
	The Dissolution of Classical Art	66
4.	**The Romantic Form of Art**	73–98
	The Aesthetic Challenge of Modernity and the Problematic of Romantic Art	73
	The Deduction of Romantic Art	74
	The Configuration of Content in Romantic Art	77
	The Romantic Construal of Religious Representation	79
	The Romantic Construal of Conduct	80
	Romantic Options in A World of Revolutionary Challenge	82
	Romantic Options in A Post-Revolutionary World	84
	The Formal Independence of Romantic Character	86
	Realism, Irony, and Non-Objectivism: The End of Romantic Art	89
	The Production and Reception of Romantic Art	92
	Romanticism and the End of Art	93
5.	**The Challenge of Conceiving the Individual Arts**	99–114
	Prerequisites for a Philosophical Theory of The Individual Arts	99
	Individuating the Arts by Physical Media	101
	Kant's Division by Analogy to Speech	104
	Hegel's Division by Appeal to the Artforms	106
	The Prospects for a Systematic Division of the Arts	11

Acknowledgments

Portions of chapters 1, 3, 4, and 5 incorporate, with modifications, separately published essays of mine. Chapter 1 contains and supplements "Rethinking the Particular Forms of Art: Prolegomena to a Rational Reconstruction of Hegel's Theory of the Artforms," *The Owl of Minerva*, Vol. 24, No. 2, Spring 1993. Chapter 3 expands upon "Hegel On Classical Art: A Reexamination," *Clio*, Vol. 24, No. 2, Winter 1995. Chapter 4 incorporates "Hegel, Romanticism, and Modernity," *The Owl of Minerva*, Vol. 27, No. 1, Fall 1995. Chapter 5 includes with minor changes "Conceiving the Individual Arts: Lessons From Kant and Hegel," *Idealistic Studies*, Vol. 26, No. 1, 1996.

Introduction

Aesthetics has three fundamental levels, corresponding to the three constitutive dimensions of art. These levels address respectively the features universal to art, specific to particular artforms, and unique to individual arts. No aesthetic phenomenon can exist without involving all three dimensions at once, for every artwork realizes the features common to art in some particular style and in an individual medium. Nevertheless, in the order of conception the determination of art in general comes first, followed by that of the particular artforms, and finally by that of the individual arts.

This conceptual succession might suggest that aesthetics would historically expend its energies first and foremost on art in general, to a lesser degree on the artforms, and to the least measure on the individual arts in function of the increasing difficulty of completing all levels of aesthetic theory in the order of their theoretical presuppositions. Yet, among the three levels of aesthetics, what has languished as the far most neglected area is the sphere of the particular artforms, where the stylistic options distinguishing cultural divides and artistic periods become thematic. Virtually all philosophies of art have investigated the generic features of aesthetic phenomena, proposing myriad theories of art in general from which analyses of style and individual arts might proceed. And a much diminished, yet still sizable contingent has ventured to characterize the different arts, either singly or, more rarely, in the totality of their division. Yet when it comes to conceiving the particular modes of artistic construal, the field is almost deserted, with few besides Schelling and Hegel[1] turning to the artforms in their own right. Indeed, figures such as Schlegel, Schiller, and Nietzsche,[2] and, in later years, Lukács, Adorno, Szondi, Benjamin, and Rosen[3] have discussed certain artforms as realized in literature, music, and other individual arts. Nonetheless, their analyses have presupposed the artforms, be it under the rubric of the naive and the sentimental, the Dionysian and the Apollonian, or the classical and the romantic, and focused instead upon how these styles take on literary or musical shape.

As a consequence, the philosophy of art has largely condemned itself to an impoverished formality, shutting itself off from offering any insight into the concrete aesthetic problems confronting artists, art critics, and the public at large. With few exceptions, philosophical analyses of art address the general features of aesthetic worth and the most basic limits of different artistic media, but otherwise remain silent on the stylistic dimensions so essential for understanding differences in culture and artistic period, as well as the fate of art in the modern world.

This relative neglect should come as no surprise given how aesthetics has been dominated by metaphysical and transcendental approaches that exclude a differentiation of artforms from rational conception and relegate treatment of style to empirical art criticism.

The metaphysical approach, pioneered by Plato and Aristotle, seeks the measure of aesthetic value in the embodiment of antecedently given intelligible forms.[4] As a result, the beauty of each and every artwork has a common pole of reference: the success with which the work of art gives sensuous representation to forms of the appropriate significance to warrant display. This guiding principle for the production, being, and reception of art applies indifferently to individual artworks. It does allow, as the example of Aristotle's *Poetics* shows, for assessing how different genres, such as the epic, the lyric, and tragedy, are suited to represent varying ranges of content. Yet since in each case, the intelligible forms worthy of artistic construal remain antecedently given, they are subject to embodiment by an indefinite plurality of artistic instances, whose aesthetic perfection will always be measured by the common standard of the given form. This leaves the individuating detail of the artwork incidental to its beauty while rendering any stylistic differences among groups of works within the same genre just as incidental to their aesthetic calibre. Moreover, since the relation between artistic construal and artistic content here always remains one of an embodiment of prior form, and the same forms are always given to art, there is no basis for any necessary differentiation of particular modes of artistic construal. It is thus no accident that purveyors of the metaphysical approach from Plato to Mao have, at most, granted polemical consideration to a plurality of artforms, as deviance warranting reduction to a single unity.

Although the transcendental turn in aesthetics, heralded by Hume and Kant, sets art free from the embodiment of given form, it substitutes a no less unitary principle from which beauty is determined: the conditions of aesthetic reception. Whether these conditions be identified empirically, as observed human psychology, given cultural frameworks, or historical institutions of an "artworld," or characterized as *a priori* structures of aesthetic judgment or aesthetic discourse, they remain the univocal determiner of aesthetic worth.[5] Hence, to the degree that anything binding can be said about objects of beauty, it will be in reference to that one and only structure from which beauty is constructed. Aesthetic worth will apply indifferently to objects of nature and products of artistry, for now what makes an appearance aesthetically significant is not its objective features, but how it is determined by the conditions of reception, whose defining role makes its structure equally underlie every aesthetic appearance. Just as the transcendental turn in epistemology renders objectivity a nature of homogeneous matter governed by laws that apply to things with indifference to their qualitative type, so beauty here becomes the undifferentiated correlate to the privileged process of aesthetic reception, leading Kant to seek its paradigmatic examples in wallpaper decoration, where questions of objective content recede into inanity.[6] By deriving the aesthetic character of art from common conditions of reception, however they be described, the transcendental approach in aesthetics can provide little else than a formal outline of appearances of beauty in general. Any differentiation of particular artforms will lie beyond the limits of transcendental constitution and fall within the contingent, corrigible labors of art historical description.

Of course, the inability of metaphysical and transcendental aesthetics to provide a philosophy of the artforms need not be cause for trouble *if* aesthetics is condemned to choose between their two alternatives. And indeed, since the great majority of aestheticians have accepted the finality of these options, they have been unperturbed to hand over treatment of the artforms to art historians. However, what prevents metaphysical and transcendental aesthetics from conceiving the artforms is precisely what sabotages their efforts to conceive art in general. What eludes the grasp of both approaches, subverting their entire efforts, is the special exemplary individuality pervading all dimensions of aesthetic phenomena. This individuality is evident in how the unique detail of an artwork is not incidental, but essential to its aesthetic significance, in how the originality of art is reflected in the subordination of artisanship to creativity in artistic production, and in how art appreciation goes astray if it seeks to judge works by appealing to externally given standards.[7] By determining aesthetic worth in function of embodying given universal forms, or in being determined by a common process of reception, the metaphysical and transcendental approaches cannot help but reduce the aesthetic dimension to a merely universal scaffold from which everything individual falls out as an unaccounted for surd. Consequently, the production, actuality, and reception of art are rendered unintelligible, lacking sufficient determinacy to distinguish them from prosaic phenomena and to lay hold of their irreducibly aesthetic character.[8]

Yet, the limits of the metaphysical and transcendental approaches are far from insurmountable. The philosophy of art can overcome the metaphysical appeal to antecedent givens and the transcendental appeal to privileged procedures of construction by paying due heed to the individuality of art and conceiving aesthetic phenomena from the outset in terms of the unity of meaning and configuration ineliminable from the being, genesis, and appreciation of beauty. When this is done, the minimal character of aesthetic worth exhibits a melding of form and content involving an independent originality simply incompatible with entities defined as either embodying given forms (in the way that an artifact materializes an antecedent blueprint shared by other instances of equivalent perfection) or deriving from a common procedure of construction. Such a unity goes beyond the limits of merely natural order, for neither the lawfulness of matter in motion, of regularity and harmony in physical and chemical processes, or of organic unity in plant and animal life can exhibit a configuration whose detail is invested with an independently significant meaning. Only the self-determined reality of free agency can provide appearances imbued with original significance, and that free agency can offer only when its own immediate existence is transfigured, freeing it and its productions from all the features that are incidental to the meaning it imposes upon itself.[9] For these reasons, the individuality of beauty lies specifically in art, rather than in nature, and in an art that presents rational agency with transfigured appearances of itself. Yet in order for these appearances to command the independent worth that goes hand in hand with the autonomy of beauty, they must present a self-understanding of rational agency that is both fundamental in significance and undisclosed by other avenues. Although science, religion, and conduct comprise the privileged domains of rational life possessing intrinsic worth, science possesses a restriction to what is universal that makes it unsusceptible of artistic construal. Hence, the content of beauty will revolve around fundamental religious and ethical truths, whose individual dimensions make them amenable to sensible, imaginative transfigurings where what is signified is tied to the original detail of its appearance.[10]

This leaves aesthetics the philosophy of fine art, whose beauty resides in exemplary imaginative configurations providing a fundamental self-understanding to humanity. Artistic creation is accordingly determined in reference to the production of such unities of meaning and shape, just as aesthetic reception is defined in terms of the process of recognizing appearances under the constitutive categories of art.

Although these considerations only begin to sketch the bare outline of what is common to art,[11] the possibility of building upon them a theory of artforms should already be clear. To the degree that artistic beauty involves an interconnection between meaning and shape, and the meaning of art lies in fundamental self-understandings of humanity, a differentiation of artforms might well arise from the conjunction of the plurality of fundamental world views and the task of creating corresponding configurations that provide unique insights into them. As long as the options are somehow conceptually determinable, the door is open for a philosophical theory of artforms that steals the thunder from art history, which would otherwise take sole possession of the analysis of artistic style.

The great pioneer in pursuing this possibility is Hegel, whose *Lectures on Aesthetics* provide a sorely forgotten guide for systematically reconceiving the philosophy of art at all three of its levels. In *Systematic Aesthetics*, I have attempted to determine art in general, critically appropriating and revising Hegel's arguments. *Stylistics: Rethinking The Artforms After Hegel* builds upon the results of that investigation, taking the conception of art in general as a point of departure for addressing the theory of the artforms.

Chapter 1 takes up the controversy over the possibility of a theory of the artforms in order to establish how the artforms can be conceived systematically and to indicate the basic division under which they are to be considered.

Chapters 2, 3, and 4 then develop in succession the three fundamental artforms, the symbolic, the classical, and the romantic.

Chapter 5 concludes the investigation by introducing the problem of moving from the theory of the artforms to the theory of the individual arts.

Throughout, Hegel's aesthetic theory is discussed in detail, not to provide an interpretation and commentary to his argument, but to enter into a critical dialogue from which a justified theory can emerge.

1

The Problem of Artistic Style: Conceiving the Particular Forms of Art

Controversies in Moving Beyond the Universal Features of Art

If aesthetics is to avoid presupposing its subject matter, it must begin by determining the universal features of the work of art, artistic creation, and the reception of art. As such, these features are ingredient in all further forms of art and every individual art. Yet, as merely universal determinations of art, they themselves do not differentiate whatever particular artforms and individual arts there may be. Indeed, if any candidate for a universal constituent of art were peculiar to a particular form or individual branch of art, it would disqualify itself as an element in the account of art in general. Conversely, a particular mode of artistic creation may necessarily incorporate those general desiderata that make something an object of art, but an artform's particularity must reside in something more, just as what distinguishes one individual art from another must lie beyond the constitutive elements common to every work of art, every artistic creation, and every aesthetic awareness.

Consequently, once the determination of art in general has been achieved, the question arises as to whether aesthetics has exhausted its enterprise, and if not, with what further dimensions of art it can and must next proceed.

If the account of the universal features of art comprised all that aesthetics could address, this would signify that everything pertaining to particular forms of art and the individual arts as such would be beyond *a priori* conceptual analysis. In that case, all examination of such themes as classical and romantic modes of art and the distinctive features of music, painting, literature and the like, would be relegated to the empirical, doxological labors of art criticism. The only conceptual resources available would be the categories determining art in general, and all art critics could do would be to apply these given concepts to the perceived reality of different historical styles and branches of art, exercising a form of judgment that could never overcome the uncertainties of interpretation.

If, however, aesthetics does not exhaust its labors in determining the reality of beauty in general, but can conceptually determine the necessary features of particular artforms and of the individual arts, how are these domains to be addressed? Should one begin with the particular forms of art or with the individual arts, and what mandates the order of treatment or the differentiation of either level of determination?

Given the immanent character of systematic argument, where any conceptual advance must rely on nothing but the terms already established, the ordering of topics will reside in their own content. Whether the determination of art in its universality is followed by the particular forms of art or the individual arts is decided by their internal relation to one another. What follows the account of art in general must be a domain that incorporates the universal features of art without already incorporating the elements specific to the domain that follows its treatment. If the particular artforms are determined prior to the individual arts, this will signify that the forms of art are distinguishable without introducing any features specific to an individual art, whereas the individual arts incorporate in their own reality the different artforms. If, conversely, the individual arts come first, this means that what differentiates individual arts from one another plays a constitutive role in defining the particular forms of art.

Hegel, for one, upholds the former ordering, proceeding from an account of what is constitutive of artistic beauty in general to the determination of the particular forms of art before addressing the individual arts. Granted that the artforms are particular, and the different artistic media are individual, this order of treatment accords with the logical analysis of universality, particularity, and individuality provided by Hegel's *Logic*. There individuality comes last since its specification rests upon the unity of universality and particularity. Although Hegel is duly aware that these categories are determined in respect to one another, he recognizes that a particular, being an undifferentiated member of a class, presupposes the universal of the class, whereas an individual, being a differentiated member of a class, presupposes both that universal and the particularity of class membership. The same ordering of internal constitution seems eminently plausible in regard to the reality of artistic beauty. Before particular forms of art, such as the classical and the romantic, can be determined, the general features of art must be ascertained that permit either the classical or the romantic to possess the common character of being forms *of art*. Similarly, before the individual arts, such as architecture, sculpture, painting, music, and literature, can be determined in their own right, both the general features of art, and the differentia of the particular modes of art, must be at hand. Otherwise, no individual art can qualify as a case of art, nor as a case that can exhibit a particular mode of artistic creation.

Nevertheless, the logic behind treating the particular prior to the individual dimension of art is obscured by the fact that Hegel tends to conflate the conceptualization of the particular forms of art with descriptions of their historical exemplifications. This gives the impression that the differentiation of artforms is a necessary sequence of epochs in the history of art. If, however, the particular forms of art are characterized in terms of the historical facticity of certain modes of artistic beauty, then they cannot fail to incorporate the individual arts, independently of which art cannot actually exist. For although, in the order of conception, the universal features of beauty may precede the particular forms of art and the individual arts, in the order of phenomenal existence, no aspect of artistic beauty can appear other than in unique creations of architecture, sculpture, painting, music, literature, or some other individual art.

An example of how understanding the particular forms of art as historical formations entails treating them not before, but after the individual arts is provided by Stephen Bungay in his study of Hegel's Aesthetics, *Beauty and Truth*.[1] Bungay differentiates the particular artforms from the individual arts by maintaining that the former constitute the "*forms of the form* of art," whereas the latter comprise the "*forms of the content* of art."[2] So differentiated, it indeed seems perplexing why the differences in form of the artforms should be considered particular, whereas the differences in content of the individual arts should be considered individual.[3] Both differences seem to be on a par, as particular differentia characterizing the existence of individual works of art. However, such a differentiation of artforms and art media in terms of form and content is itself suspect. Due to the interrelation of meaning and shape basic to art, any particular forms of art and any individual arts will equally be defined by their own constellations of both form and content. Indeed, as will be seen, the philosophical treatment of these concrete dimensions of art will focus upon how they further particularize and individuate the aesthetic relation of meaning and configuration.

What compounds Bungay's oversight is that he interprets the particular forms of art as historical cultural unities comprising the forms in which different world views gain artistic expression in the historical development of humanity.[4] Accordingly, he criticizes Hegel for treating these forms prior to the individual arts, maintaining that the whole doctrine of particular artforms is a heterogeneous pastiche best dismembered into one remain falling within the universal dimension of art and another falling into the system of arts. For, on the one hand, the differentiation of artforms revolves around the purely universal issue of the logical relation between form and content, whose possibilities fall within the account of artistic beauty in general. And, on the other hand, besides the truism that art embodies beliefs that vary through time, everything else attaching to the *historical* reality of artforms falls into the cornucopia of given facticity better left to historians and critics.[5] Since this eliminates any mediating particular dimension between the universal features of art and the individual arts, Bungay concludes that the arts are particular, whereas the individual domain of art consists in actual works of art as they are sociologically and historically given. The individual dimension of art thereby falls beyond the reach of systematic philosophy into the hands of critical interpretation and historical scholarship.[6]

Admittedly, works of art are concrete instances, realizing as individuals the conceptual determinations that aesthetics establishes as constitutive for art. Granted, too, that the particular artforms can come into existence as historical periods of artistic style. However, that art works are individuals does not preclude the different arts from exhibiting individuality in themselves. To be individual, the different arts must incorporate universal and particular factors, for, as the logic of individuality teaches, the unique class membership constitutive of the individual is parasitic upon the universality of the class and the particularity of undifferentiated class membership. In the case of the arts, the universal factors are already provided by the account of artistic beauty in general. If the artforms are conceived not as given cultural phenomenon, infested with the individuality of historical existence, but as particular modes of artistic reality, whose actual realization entails additional features, the artforms can possess their identifying character without reference to any specific artistic media. Then they can supply particular factors helping enable the different arts to be individual. Together, the features making something a work of art in general and those making it a particular form of art supply everything needed for an art to qualify as an undifferentiated member of the class of arts. The further determination of what is peculiar to one medium in contrast to another will provide the additional individuating factor, marking off one media as a unique member of the class of arts, granted the concomitant contribution of the general and particular features that make such class membership possible in the first place.

Moreover, to claim that the only individuality of art lies in actual singular works is at odds with the universal determination of beauty. For, as we have seen, the category of individuality is basic to every aspect of art in general.

All these reasons underscore how the forms of art are determinable as particular modes of artistic creation, independently of the individual arts. However, it still seems possible that the individual arts, for their part, are determinable without reference to the particular artforms. To distinguish painting from architecture, for instance, does not involve the forms of art, especially when, as particular, the artforms can inhere in each and every individual art. Since painting and architecture can presumably both be classical or romantic in form, what differentiates one artistic medium from the other must be sought elsewhere.

Why not then follow Bungay and treat the different arts as particular types of art, differentiated according to their media, without, on the other hand, following his lead of dismissing the artforms as particular modes in their own right? In that case, the different arts and the different artforms would appear to be equiprimordial, with each set able to qualify the other. An art, such as music, could be further qualified by being subsumed under the classical or romantic forms, just as an artform, such as the symbolic, could be further qualified according to the art in which it inheres. On this understanding, the individual arts would comprise particular modes of the artforms just as the forms of art would comprise particular modes of the individual arts. It would then be a matter of indifference whether aesthetics addressed the artforms before the individual arts. If the artforms came first, then the specification of the individual arts would proceed by conceiving each art in general and then in terms of the different forms by which it brings the artistic modes to existence. If the individual arts were considered to be prior, then the account of the artforms would proceed by examining each form of art per se and then in respect to its embodiment in every type of media. In each case, the artforms and arts would be considered in their own right and then they would be addressed in their interaction, where artforms are modified in respect to their embodiment in the different arts and the different arts get differentiated according to their realizations of each of the artforms. Then, artforms and art would each figure as particular and individual. The artforms would be particular in respect to their individuated realization in each art (e.g., as musical as opposed to literary realizations of the classical), just as each art would be particular in respect to its different artform embodiments (e.g., as classical in distinction from romantic music). Alternately, each artform would be individual as a unique member of the class of artforms, just as each art would be an individuated instance of an art medium.

As whole, the determination of the artforms and arts would thereby advance in two major stages. First, they would each be determined in general as coeval particularizations of art, where it would be a matter of indifference which would be conceived before the other. Secondly, they would then be determined in terms of how they individuate one another, whereby what is generic to the artforms would be combined with what is generic to each art to differentiate every art in respect to its realizations of each artform and to differentiate every artform in respect to its realization in each art. Again, it would make no difference which differentiation is pursued first, since, in effect, each is equivalent to the other.

Yet, on closer examination, does the presumed reciprocity sustain itself? Whereas the different artforms can inhere in different artistic media, can the different arts inhere in the forms of art? It may be that an art, such as music, cannot exist without taking the form of a unique composition exhibiting one of the artforms, such as classical or romantic, that other works of this and other arts will share. And, by the same token, an artform, such as the classical, admittedly cannot exist without being embodied in a creation of a specific artistic medium. Nevertheless, can the arts be features of the artforms? Do they not rather comprise real media, not devoid of character in the way in which matter could be considered only potential in respect to the form that gives it determinate actuality, but already formed in terms of their own material way of joining meaning and configuration? This would reflect how, in relation to the artforms, the arts are individual, whereas, in relation to the individual arts, the forms of art represent particular modes of their existence.

Important methodological ramifications would follow from this ordering. The determination of the artforms would, to begin with, depend upon a differentiation of particular modes by means of factors constitutive of art in general. Then, each particular artform would be determinable in virtue of how its differentiating factors further qualify the way in which each universal feature of art is realized in that form. Accordingly, all the basic themes of the conception of art in general would reintroduce themselves so that the reality of the work of art, artistic creation, and aesthetic appreciation would be conceived as they are transfigured in this or that artform.

When, finally, the individual arts are determined, the process would take on a double complication. In accord with systematic immanence, the factors minimally distinguishing one art from another would have to be found in prior determinations. Yet, once these factors have been identified, the determination of each art would proceed in a twofold manner. On the one hand, each art would be determined in incorporating the general features of artistic beauty in respect to its specific medium. This would identify what is peculiar to a certain medium of the reality of the work of art, its artistic creation, and its appreciation. On the other hand, each art would be further internally differentiated in view of incorporating the particular artforms as they are modified in attaining realization in the medium in question. In this way, how a specific art takes on, for the sake of argument, a symbolic, classical, or romantic form, would be determined. At each juncture, the necessary resources would have to be provided not by appeals to observed phenomena of art history, but by integrating conceptual determinations of art that have already been established.

These observations are all anticipatory judgments that take for granted the differentiations of artforms and art media. From a systematic point of view, only the subsequent account can certify that they are conceivable and that they conform to the ordering that has been suggested by their putative characterizations.

In line with that further development, what first must be established are the factors ingredient in artistic beauty in general that allow for further particularization.

The Artforms as Minimal Particularizations of Art

Given how art constitutively involves a unity of meaning and configuration, manifesting in sensuous and imaginative form truths providing a fundamental self-understanding to a rational audience, two parallel avenues present themselves for particularizing the reality of artistic beauty.

At first glance, it would appear that these paths consist in differentiating, on the one hand, types of self-understanding or world view that comprise the component of meaning in artistic beauty, and on the other hand, types of configuration that shape these contents. These dual differentiations could only be carried out as discrete operations if the kinds of world views were determined independently of the types of configuration. In that case, the typology of outlooks would have no specific relation to problems of artistic configuration, whereas the sorting of configurations would proceed in terms of purely formal considerations without regard for the content of art.

Such formal taxonomies of content, on the one hand, and of configuration, on the other, have, of course, frequently been pursued by historians of art, as well as by aesthetic thinkers. Art has been typed as bourgeois or proletarian, for example, by many Marxist critics in virtue of the economic interests art allegedly expresses, just as art has been differentiated as Christian, Islamic, Judaic, Hindu, and so forth according to the religious doctrine art portrays. Analogously, figures such as Heinrich Wölfflin have differentiated art into linear versus painterly, closed versus open, composite versus fused, and other such polar types, building a morphology of style developed in indifference to the content of artistic configuration.[7]

Hegel himself engages in such formal taxonomy when he distinguishes between the so-called severe, ideal, and pleasing styles of art in his introduction to the analysis of the individual arts.[8] These styles are distinguished by the degree of freedom they exhibit in mastering the external form of the work of art, in express abstraction from the specific meaning of the work or the particular artform or individual art to which it belongs.[9] Allegedly, the severe style expresses its content with a minimum of ornament and expression, the ideal style treats its content with a grace and liveliness in which the external form is not dominated by its meaning, but freely and harmoniously expressive of it, and the pleasing style goes to the extreme of setting the detail of configuration free of its meaning in appeal to the subjective gratification of the audience.[10]

The problem with all such typologies is not just that they are at a loss to distinguish themselves from ad hoc accommodations to contingent historical phenomena, but that they proceed in indifference and even in contradiction to the fundamental unity of the work of art. Precisely because artistic beauty lies in the wedding of form and content, any analysis that sorts the configurations of art or the meanings of art in independence from one another ignores the specifically aesthetic element of each. Instead, the differentiation of artistically conveyed outlooks needs to proceed in conjunction with a differentiation of the configurations that are specifically linked to each world view. Their differentiation cannot comprise two separate taxonomies, but rather a single specification where what is actually at issue are kinds of unity of the meaning and shape of art, where each type involves the particular relation of its own specific world view and corresponding form of configuration.[11]

Consequently, the particularization of art can proceed, at least in one regard, as a differentiation of the unity of meaning and configuration into possible types. Since, however, this differentiation determines its modes of configuration without regard for the particular type of material that they employ, the sensuous character of the art object provides a basis for a correlative avenue of particularization. Namely, the external medium by which the unity of meaning and shape is made manifest can itself be differentiated into possible types. The former alternative of distinguishing modes of aesthetic unity would correspond to a taxonomy of artforms, whereas the latter differentiation of media would correspond to a typology of arts.

Significantly, distinguishing different types of aesthetic unity requires no other resources than the concepts of meaning and shape already at hand in the determination of artistic beauty and the work of art. By contrast, distinguishing different arts requires introducing physical and spiritual differences such as those between visibility and audibility, between fixity and change in time and space, and between mute sensations and language. Admittedly, all of these factors are implied by the basic reality of artistic beauty to the extent that it involves tangible creations of and for sentient rational individuals. However, these factors still have not yet figured in their distinctive differences as determining elements of aesthetic reality. Hence, there is a divergence in what artforms and arts require for their specification. Owing to this divergence, the differentiation of types of aesthetic unity (i.e., of artforms) can be incorporated within the differentiation of media (i.e., the arts) without further additions, whereas the differentiation of media cannot be incorporated within the differentiation of types of aesthetic unity without introducing the physical and spiritual factors cited earlier. In this respect, types of aesthetic unity are more rudimentary than types of artistic media and thus provide a more minimal particularization of artistic beauty. On this account, the artforms can precede the individual arts as a topic of systematic aesthetics, even though the differentiation of artistic media per se does not depend on that of the forms of art.

How then can types of aesthetic unity be determined in any *a priori* and complete manner? As we have seen, the individuality of artistic beauty entails that the meaning of a work of art be uniquely connected to the shape by which it appears. Can there still be particular modes of this connection, modes that can be distinguished according to some principle certifying the necessity and exhaustive character of their specification? Although the content and form of art must always stand wedded to one another, their relation can take three conceivable forms. The content may

(1) contain a meaning too abstract to be directly manifest in any sensuous configuration, or
(2) it may mean something that can be exhaustively presented in sensuous form, or
(3) it may convey a truth too concrete to be limited to any particular shape.

These options have a logical completeness in that meaning and shape can fit or diverge, and if they do diverge, they can do so in either of two directions, where, in one case, meaning falls short of shape, and, in the other, shape falls short of meaning.

Nevertheless, this differentiation might appear suspect in two respects. First, the case where meaning and shape are congruent seems to represent the general unity of form and content intrinsic to artistic beauty, whereas the two cases of a discrepancy between meaning and configuration seem to violate the individuality of art, disrupting the wedding of universal significance and its particularization. In other words, the supposed differentiation of artforms is no differentiation at all, since only one "form" qualifies as art and does so by being what is generic to art rather than by being a particular species of artistic beauty.

On the other hand, the distinction between the two forms of discrepancy does not seem to rest on differences in the relation between meaning and shape. As Bungay maintains in critiquing Hegel's differentiation of artforms, the same relation of non-identity is present in both cases; what distinguishes them is not the form-content relation, but rather differences in the meaning present in each. And since such differences in content can be indeterminately manifold, all that properly can be said is that there can be at least two different artforms, one in which form and content are in identity, and one in which they are not. That there be only two types of non-identity is an arbitrary restriction blind to the heterogeneous possibilities of content.[12]

Do these two objections really hold? As Hegel's entire accounts of symbolic and romantic artforms are at pains to substantiate, it is far from self-evident that an incongruence in meaning and shape undermines the individuality and unity of form and content constitutive of aesthetic worth. The truth that a work of art expresses may well be so abstract in character that the configuration that conveys it must point beyond itself in order to make it manifest. Nonetheless, the configuration that achieves this self-transcending service may still be uniquely suited to do so, providing a novel image that imaginatively intimates a humane truth too devoid of particular content to be given an immediate shape. In the converse case, which Hegel ascribes to the romantic artform, where the self-understanding to be conveyed is too concrete to be confined to the particular limits of any specific configuration, there may equally be a unique shape that does specifically point to such a meaning, retaining the aesthetic connection of form and content. These options need to be spelled out, as does the option of simple congruence, but their conceivability at least suggests that the artistic unity of meaning and shape might take on a variety of forms.

By the same token, there is no reason to assume that the dichotomy of identity and non-identity exhausts the *a priori* options for connecting form and content in art. The polar discrepancies of shape and meaning may both exhibit non-identity, but that does not signify that their common non-identity cannot be further distinguished into two very different form-content relationships. Moreover, the connection of meaning and shape is hardly indifferent to their content, since the nature of the relation rests precisely upon the respective character of these relata.

On both accounts, then, the road remains open for addressing the possible modes of aesthetic unity.

The Ordering of the Artforms

Granted that there be a plurality of artforms, how should their conception be ordered and what significance does their sequence have?

Historically speaking, the few thinkers who have addressed particular forms of art as topics of aesthetics have tended to portray them as modes of artistic expression that dominate the entire artistic production of a particular culture at one period of its development, and that succeed one another in an irreversible order as historical cultural formations.[13] Hegel does this in describing the symbolic form as the governing mode of Oriental art, the classical form as the defining unity of ancient Greek art, and the romantic form as the pervading artistic mode of modern Western civilization. In so doing, he appears to presume that these artforms cannot coexist within a single culture, and that their historical sequence is both non-arbitrary and irreversible. In line with these presumptions, Hegel presents his successive treatment of the symbolic, classical, and romantic forms as a necessary progression in which the order of conception and the order of existence coincide.[14]

Something similar is at hand in Schiller's differentiation of naive and sentimental art, and in Schelling's appropriation of this categorization of artforms.[15] In both their cases, the succession of naive and sentimental forms of art is portrayed as a historical sequence, where naive art characterizes ancient culture and sentimental art typifies the productions of modernity.[16]

However, if, systematically speaking, the resources for an *a priori* differentiation of forms of art must be found in factors ingredient in art in general, and more specifically, in the relation between meaning and configuration in the work of art, can any of these assumptions be upheld?

To begin with, is there any compelling reason why a form of art should exclusively dominate the contemporaneous artistic creations of a culture, or, for that matter, even the production of a single artist? The content of art may indeed involve a world view framing the ethical conflict given exemplary shape in the art object. Moreover, there may be general types of world views that are inherently expressible in certain kinds of artistic configuration. Yet these points do not mandate that all artists of a certain culture must share the same world view, nor that an individual artist cannot experience shifts of world-view that gain expression in a body of work exhibiting different artforms. A culture may have its identity in common religious and ethical beliefs, shared customs, and accepted conventions of artistic production, just as belonging to a culture may involve an exposure and participation in such common affairs. Still, no such unities can preclude the possibility that not all arts will equally reflect the dominant outlook of their time,[17] or that artists be able and willing to choose novel or departed modes of expression and break the prevailing mold, or that each and every culture contain its artistic dissidents, or that artists change their style during their career, or that even single works of art possess parts in different styles.[18] Moreover, the degree of constancy in artistic production presupposed by any talk of forms of art does not prevent world views and corresponding styles from undergoing continuous variation, not only rendering meaningless the historical question of when one period ends and another begins,[19] but allowing for the coexistence of clashing forms representing old and new. And nothing in the conditions of artistic creation prevents artists from working in isolation, oblivious to or ignorant or forgetful of current and past traditions, or for whole cultures to develop in varying disregard for their predecessors' and contemporaries' world views and artistic achievements.

If this is the case, and no other factors intervene, then the different artforms remain contemporary possibilities at all times and places, even when one variety may dominate the others. Accordingly, the modes of unifying artistic form and content cannot masquerade as historical formations, connected in any necessary temporal sequence. They may be exemplified historically in a succession of cultural periods, but that fact will be a contingent matter that cannot dictate where, when, and how they must arise. All that can be said is that *if* an artist gives artistic expression to a certain type of world view, a certain type of configuration in a certain type of relation to the meaning it conveys will be most aesthetically appropriate.[20]

Yet, if the artforms are rooted in the logical possibilities of relating the meaning and shape of artistic beauty, and on that basis lack exclusive sovereignty over the art works of a particular cultural age, as well as over the corpus of an individual artist, are they stripped of all necessary succession? Although no artform can be guaranteed personal or communal hegemony, could there still not be a relation among them where one form constitutively incorporates elements of or refers to another and thereby presupposes its presence? Then, the appearance of one form could require the concurrent or past existence of another and, in that respect, manifest a necessary ordering. This would be true even if individual artists and cultures practiced more than one artform in the same epoch, or switched from one to another in varying directions. Certain artforms would then still be predicated upon others, whereas one would be prior to all in the order of constitution.

Some such relation could provide grounds for conceiving the artforms in a non-arbitrary order. Without such constitutive connections, the different artforms would appear to be coeval possibilities of artistic expression, whose order of conception and order of realization would be equally contingent.

The Hierarchy of Artforms and the End of Art

As is well known, Hegel not only suggests that the artforms exclusively define different cultural epochs in a necessary historical succession, but that they stand in a normative hierarchy of a twofold character. On the one hand, Hegel maintains that since the ideal of artistic beauty resides in the unity of meaning and shape, the one artform that brings these sides into a perfect congruence, the classical, is the most beautiful. On the other hand, Hegel equally argues that romantic art is most satisfactory in its revelation of truth, since the truest world view recognizes that humanity cannot be fully exhibited in any particular form and romantic art gives shape to just such an outlook.[21]

Since Hegel interprets modernity to contain the very outlook in which humanity is recognized in its universality, he is brought to a twofold conclusion regarding the historical fate of art. On the one hand, the modern age has brought the development of artforms to an end by fostering the last of the three possible forms of art. This does not preclude that artists will continue to produce works in all the different media. It means instead that no new work of art can introduce a fundamentally novel artform since the basic variations in the relation of meaning and shape have been exhausted. On the other hand, modernity has displaced art from the center of culture because the modern outlook construes the truths of humanity such that only the universal element of philosophical thought can adequately lay hold of their content. Consequently, although romantic art may be a superior artform in respect to the truth of the outlook to which it gives artistic shape, it renders art itself less significant than does the classical form, whose world view remains attached to given particulars whose exemplary stature can be most adequately captured in a work of art.

The hierarchy in Hegel's proposals raises several problems. To begin with, Hegel's elegizing of classical art as the acme of the ideal of artistic beauty seems to undermine the relation between the features of art in general and those of the artforms, as well as threaten the standing of the symbolic and romantic forms of art. The privileging of the classical form does both by suggesting that the unity of meaning and shape is only fully at hand in classical art. This undercuts the universality of the ideal of artistic beauty by identifying it with the distinguishing features of a particular artform. It equally undermines the aesthetic character of the symbolic and romantic forms by implying that they lack the thoroughgoing correlation of content and configuration generic to artistic beauty.

These problems can readily be avoided by simply refraining from treating the immediate correspondence of meaning and shape allegedly peculiar to classical art as possessing any normative primacy in relation to beauty in general. Since all artforms must, as such, share in everything generic to artistic beauty, the differences in how they connect form and content may define distinct *types* of beauty, but not a scale of different *degrees* of beauty.

Hegel, himself, acknowledges the consequences of these difficulties. He admits that a normative ranking of artforms that deems some inadequate in comparison with the true ideal of artistic beauty cannot involve any condemnation of artistic failure, as when unsuccessful works of art fail to express anything of significance, or fail to supply a configuration corresponding to what they are supposed to represent. As art, Hegel recognizes, each particular form is always adequate to the content it gives itself. If any deficiency can be spoken of at all, it must refer only to how a particular artform presents a relatively untrue determinacy in which humanity encounters itself.[22]

Thus, eliminating the misguided hierarchy in beauty still allows for a hierarchy in truth, which, in Hegel's case, reaches its climax in the dual claim that romantic art, by its specific constellation of meaning and shape, diminishes its own cultural role in its very attainment of the valid truth of humanity. Romantic art may be just as beautiful as classical art. Yet romantic art may configure a fully adequate self-conception of humanity that is best articulated in the prose of philosophical thought, whereas an outlook that views the good as inherently exemplary can encounter that truth no more completely than in classical art.

However, to sustain this hierarchy of cultural importance and truth, certain underlying assumptions must be upheld. To begin with, it must be established that there are basic types of world view that can be specified by reason for subsequent incorporation in the differentiation of artforms. Secondly, it must be demonstrated that these outlooks can be ranked according to their truth.[23] These tasks fall outside aesthetic inquiry proper into the philosophy of mind and ethics. However, if aesthetics is to be able to categorize the forms of art by particularizing the meaning and shape of artistic beauty, it must draw upon these antecedent investigations just as proved necessary in determining the content of artistic beauty.[24]

The notion of the end of art can be sustained with or without the affirmation of this latter hierarchy of artforms. So long as the constellations of the meaning and shape of artistic beauty fall into certain ***a priori*** forms, art can be said to have come to an end whenever all of these forms have come to be in history. This end of art will then simply signify that artistic creation has already produced every conceivable type of artform and that new works will only follow in the paths that have been tread before. If, in addition, the artforms do fall into a hierarchy with respect to the truth of the outlooks they configure, and to their corresponding cultural importance, the end of art will further signify that art has become a secondary vehicle of self-understanding where those artforms are practiced that undercut their own importance. Given how the differentiation of artforms is not an ordering of a necessary historical sequence, there can be no assurance that the "end of art" will have the final word.[25] It may just as well be followed by historical periods where forms of art resurface that command the highest esteem as revelations of humane truth.

All these speculations can only be adjudicated by conceiving the artforms themselves and accounting for their differentiation. To this end, Hegel's analysis of symbolic, classical, and romantic art can serve as a heuristic guide to a rational reconstruction of the forms of art, provided his intimations of historical necessity and cultural univocity are called into question.

The Logical Differentiation of the Forms of Art

The aesthetic unity of meaning and configuration can take three general forms. The self-understanding of humanity[26] conveyed by art can match or not match the shape it is given, and if no match occurs, two types of discrepancy are possible. On the one hand, the meaning can be too abstract to fit any imaginative configuration and, on the other hand, the meaning can be too concrete to be reducible to any particular shape. Hegel takes these exhaustive logical options as the basis for differentiating the forms of art, appealing to them to guarantee both the rational necessity and the completeness of his proposed division of symbolic, classical, and romantic types of art.

If we are to draw upon Hegel's conception of the particular artforms in order to reconstruct them in accord with the demands of systematic immanence, we must examine to what extent his description of artforms actually arises out of the possible options by which meaning and configuration are conjoined in the work of art.[27] This involves not only considering the identifying features ascribed to each artform, but also investigating the claims that Hegel makes concerning their order in conception as well as in reality. What complicates matters is that Hegel differentiates each form of art into a sequential system of shapes of its own.

Nevertheless, Hegel does provide us with a basic taxonomy distinguishing each artform in general that can be addressed, at least in a preliminary fashion, before considering the order of the forms of art or their internal division into further particular kinds.

The Basic Taxonomy of the Symbolic, Classical, and Romantic Forms of Art

Hegel attempts to characterize the symbolic form of art in terms of the one extreme of a discrepancy between meaning and configuration where the meaning is too abstract to fit any sensuous image. His key claim is that such a discrepancy in shape and meaning entails a symbolic form of art where a self-understanding of humanity *seeks* to make itself artistically manifest, without being able to find an adequate display. The basic argument leading to this characterization runs as follows: Because the constitutive world view of symbolic art conceives what is of essential importance to humanity in universals of an abstract and indeterminate character, its truth cannot be found in the given reality of nature or in the actual affairs of rational agents. The appearance of these domains is fundamentally alien to such truth due to their ineradicable concreteness. Yet, since art involves the wedding of meaning and sensuous configuration, symbolic art must employ images in such a way as to convey the very incongruence that they possess as vehicles for manifesting the abstract and indeterminate truth of the "symbolic" world view. Symbolic art is therefore characterized by an employment of images, which, when drawn from the given reality of natural and conventional life, can only be utilized in an arbitrary way that corrupts and distorts their given shapes.[28] As a particularization of art, the symbolic form must still, therein, achieve a conformity of meaning and shape, where the individual detail of a work's sensuous configuration is constitutively tied to the expression of its significance. However, because the shape conveys a self-understanding too abstract to have any corresponding sensuous embodiment, the accord between meaning and configuration is itself an abstract harmony in which their relation exhibits both an affinity and a mutual incompatibility. Because of this indwelling tension, the meaning of symbolic art appears as ever *seeking* its expression in the work of art, yet never finding a configuration in which it is at home.[29] This characterization has much in common with the traditional account of the sublime, and hence, it should not come as a surprise that Hegel will describe symbolic art, at least in certain of its forms, as an art of the sublime.[30]

Significantly, when Hegel identifies the abstract character of the world view generic to symbolic art, he generally describes it as an outlook that ties the "absolute" to natural entities lacking the full-fledged subjectivity of rational agency. Since such natural factors are too impoverished in "spiritual" resources to exhibit the truth of humanity that is conferred upon them, that truth is left underdetermined, and, indeed, indeterminate, insofar as the natural entities that should supply it with content cannot manifest what it should be. Hence, the meaning seeking expression in symbolic art is rendered ineffable in its own right, with none of its sensuous expressions sufficient to identify it unambiguously. When the symbolic form is addressed, it must be established whether the abstract character of its meaning is intrinsically wedded to such natural determination or whether it represents only one of its forms.

In contrast to the symbolic form, Hegel construes classical art as no longer merely seeking an expression for its meaning, but rather finding a perfectly adequate artistic shape for the world view it takes as essential. Determined as the artform embodying the logical possibility of a conformity in truth and configuration, classical art must satisfy a dual requirement. On the one hand, it must present a self-understanding of humanity that can be exhaustively manifest in a sensuous shape and, on the other hand, it must employ a configuration that immediately and completely exhibits that self-understanding. Accordingly, in the classical form, the topic of art, the valued strivings of rational agency, must be construed as fundamentally individual and not as a merely universal abstraction. However, the individuality essential to humanity must not be one that has its identity in an inner life transcending any external entanglement. In that case, any congruence between meaning and shape would once more become problematic. Rather, rational agency must be construed as having an individuality tied to a particular sensible reality, from which nothing of significance remains concealed.[31] Moreover, since natural factors are insufficient to provide an adequate content for the self-understanding of humanity, the truth to be expressed must be freed of restrictions to natural forms lacking the capabilities of rational agency.

The vision of humanity conforming to this mandate is one that construes the valid reality of rational agency to lie in the external appearance of humane conduct instead of in brute nature, transcendent ideals, or the hidden sanctum of inner life. For its part, the configuration that can transparently reveal this self-understanding will consist in the actual physical appearance of rational agents, imaginatively transfigured so that everything on the surface is invested with the appropriate meaning. Accordingly, classical art will focus upon the living, bodily reality of free individuals, whose activities are fundamentally imbued with a universality that is no less particularized and thereby wedded to its specific manifestation. This allows the external existence presented by art to shed any remaining independence over and against the meaning it conveys, just as it permits the expressed self-understanding to have only itself and all of itself manifest in the configuration at hand.[32] Consequently, classical art does not *re-present* a meaning that has some independently given shape. Rather, it *presents* that meaning in a configuration in which it originally and immediately dwells.[33]

Finally, Hegel develops romantic art as the form defined by the remaining possible relation of meaning and shape, that where the self-understanding on display is too concrete to be limited to a particular sensuous configuration. Here the separation of content and form is reintroduced, but in a way that reverses the discrepancy putatively underlying symbolic art. Whereas the symbolic form of art configures a self-understanding of humanity that is too abstract to be univocally manifest in any sensuous configuration, the romantic form exhibits an outlook that can be partially exhibited in different shapes, but cannot be limited to any one sensuous realization. It presents a self-understanding that conceives the essence of rational agency to lie in an autonomy overcoming any restriction to specific external appearances while engrossed in determining itself. As such, the shapes employed by romantic art are rendered indifferent to the meaning they express. This indifference, however, is not a reversion to symbolic art's equivocal relation of appearances that point beyond themselves to an ineffable sublimity. It rather comprises a new relation where sensuous configurations exhibit the soul-searching of an autonomous humanity, whose problems and strivings are never fully realized in any given shape.[34] Accordingly, whereas symbolic art *seeks* an elusive unity of meaning and configuration, and classical art *finds* the perfect match in a sensuously defined individuality, romantic art *transcends* the unity of form and content, all the while from within the confine of artistic beauty.[35]

Such are the basic features that Hegel ascribes to the three artforms in function of the three alternative relations of meaning and configuration in the work of art.

The legitimacy of these differentiations has, of course, been called into question, starting with Hegel's younger contemporaries, Ch. H. Weisse, von Ulrici, and Friedrich Theodor Vischer, whose critiques have recently been given new life by Vittorio Hösle.[36] Their common objection is that Hegel offers a deficiently linear progression, ignoring the "dialectical" resolution an additional artform would achieve by uniting the subjective and objective elements of art still left unreconciled by the romantic form.[7] Hösle argues that only such a revision could comprehend Renaissance art, which otherwise, he maintains, falls outside the reach of the romantic art form.[37] However, if the allegedly missing artform is construed as unifying objectivity and subjectivity, how can it be distinguished from classical art, whose congruent unity of meaning and configuration permits a naturally determined self-understanding of humanity to be adequately objectified in a sensuous form? And if Renaissance art involves something more than the classical ideal, is it not a humanistic vision of rational agency, freeing the creative spirit to transcend any particular sensuous limitation, while ennobling the most mundane human pursuits? Far from challenging the boundaries of romantic construal, Renaissance art would then only fall within its borders.

A systematic critique of the artforms must turn away from such extraneous considerations of "dialectical" versus "linear" orderings and their nostalgia for classical harmonies. Instead, attention must focus upon the features constitutively particularizing artistic construal, examining in this light to what degree Hegel's taxonomy of symbolic, classical, and romantic art both exhausts and properly characterizes the possibilities.

To evaluate the characterizations of these putative artforms, it is difficult to avoid addressing the system of variations into which Hegel differentiates each one. These are presented not only as exhausting the possible options within the particular form of art to which they belong. They are equally conceived as progressively transforming their defining constellation of meaning and shape until it mutates into a new type of art, or, in the case of romantic art, beyond art into prosaic modes of self-understanding. Systematically speaking, the relation between the artforms should be something internal to their own conceptual constitution, rather than something externally imposed. Hence, any analysis of the ordering and interconnection of Hegel's proposals for the forms of art can ill afford to ignore entirely his differentiations of each type.

As it turns out, each proposed form of art poses conceptual problems in regard to its relation to the determinations of art in general, as well as to its relation to the other artforms. Nevertheless, for the purpose of reconstructing systematic aesthetics, we can fruitfully draw upon the characterizations that Hegel has given these three forms of art, provided we subject them to a critique that always keeps in view the requirements of categorial immanence.

2

The Symbolic Form of Art

Preliminary Difficulties in Characterizing the Symbolic Form of Art

In the aftermath of Hegel, any attempt to determine the symbolic form of art must grapple with the two intersecting ambiguities that plague Hegel's characterization. On the one hand, Hegel presents the symbolic form as coming first both in the order of conception and in the order of realization. On the other hand, Hegel describes symbolic art as lying at the threshold of fine art proper, as if the symbolic discrepancy between meaning and configuration lay outside the unity of artistic beauty, as its deficient harbinger.[1] Each of these views is couched, at times, in the form of a systematic a priori claim[2] and, at other times, in the manner of an empirical interpretation of observed history. How is the symbolic form of art to be determined systematically in light of these possible options?

If symbolic art is addressed first not for convenience's sake as one among other conceptually coeval forms, but as the topic with which the theory of artforms must begin, a dual requirement must be met. Coming first in the order of conception, the symbolic form should neither incorporate any features specific to the classical and romantic artforms, nor should they be conceivable apart from its distinctive properties. The symbolic form should be the most rudimentary of them all and the other forms should be predicated upon it, enjoying their own constellations of meaning and configuration only by either incorporating or making reference to aspects of symbolic art.

These requirements must be further supplemented if the symbolic form is also to be first in the order of realization. Then, not only must the conception of classical and romantic art depend upon the incorporation or reference to the concept of symbolic art, but the actual existence of these artforms must be preceded by the appearance of symbolic art. Symbolic art could still possibly be produced once again after the advent of classical and romantic creations, either in ignorance of the latter forms or in express rejection of their development. Yet, any further production of classical or romantic art works would always have to be preceded by the existence of symbolic creations.

It might appear that the order in realization of artforms follows directly from the order in conception insofar as if one artform is defined by incorporating aspects of another, it cannot come to be unless those aspects are already given in reality. Yet, that one artform cannot exist unless its ingredients are at hand does not mandate that the conceptually prior artform have an antecedent independent realization of its own. The more rudimentary form certainly can exist without bringing into being the additional features that conceptually subsequent artforms bring to bear when they incorporate the former in their own constitution. However, the conceptually subsequent forms of art could conceivably be created without any antecedently existing examples of symbolic art, provided their creators succeed in implanting those features that can be independently realized in the symbolic form.

Compounding the challenge of substantiating the conceptual and historical priority of symbolic art is the problem of upholding the discrepancy of meaning and configuration defining the symbolic form without overturning the unity of form and content basic to artistic beauty. When Hegel discusses how art does indeed originally come into existence by taking the symbolic form, he equivocally links the conceptual and historical priority of symbolic art to the issue of fitting symbolic art within the parameters of artistic beauty. On the one hand, Hegel characterizes symbolic art as the form in which art originates, while, on the other hand, he suggests that symbolic art comprises the prehistory of art, paving the way for the unity of meaning and shape that the classical form of art will first be able to establish.[3] Complicating matters further, he even suggests that the symbolic artform undergoes its own development from threshold to starting point of art.[4] Can the symbolic form straddle both the prehistory and the beginning of art, and indeed, can symbolic art then count as art at all?

Fully resolving whether symbolic art has either a conceptual or historical priority cannot be accomplished without determining the other artforms and ascertaining to what extent they incorporate aspects of symbolic art and depend upon its antecedent existence. However, certain underpinnings of this priority can, and must, be addressed independently of accounting for classical and romantic art. If symbolic art is to come first in conception or in reality, then it should be determinable in its own right without appeal to the concepts or existence of classical and romantic art. Moreover, if symbolic art is to qualify as a genuine artform that also comes first into existence, it must fall within art proper as its starting point, rather than receding back into art's prehistory.

To understand to what extent these requirements can be and are met, the role of the symbol in symbolic art must first be delineated.

The Role of the Symbol in Symbolic Art

As Hegel points out, if the symbol is to enter into the account of artforms, it must do so only in respect to how it serves as a differentiating mode for artistic expression. What is irrelevant is how the symbol may figure as an incidental appendage leaving undetermined the particular type to which an entire work of art belongs. Symbols may well play such a role in classical and romantic art works or figure in purely prosaic artifacts. However, the symbol, as it defines the symbolic form of art, must command a central role, determining how the work it informs falls into one rather than another artform.[5]

In order to comprehend the determining role of the symbol in symbolic art, the features that set the symbol apart from other representations must first be identified. The symbol is a sign, and as such, it contains two dimensions: a meaning, comprising the idea or topic it conveys, and the expression, comprising the perceivable appearance by which it presents that content. However, as Hegel observes, whereas a sign can unite its meaning and expression in a completely arbitrary fashion, where what the expression means is entirely unrelated to that expression's sensuous shape, in the symbol the arbitrariness of the linkage is overcome. Unlike the mere sign, the symbol expresses its meaning in an image that is not indifferent to its sense. If it were, the symbol could play no determining role in art, for meaning would then be entirely extraneous to its expression in total opposition to art's constitutive kinship of meaning and configuration.[6] Instead of being a completely arbitrary sign, the symbol possesses a sensuous appearance that contains in itself[7] the meaning that it serves to express.

Yet, the expression of the symbol is not and cannot be identical to what it means, since otherwise the distinction of meaning and expression would collapse, eliminating the constitutive semiotic contrast on which the symbol and all other signs depend. As Hegel puts it, the symbol expresses not itself, but only one distinguishable aspect of its own perceivable existence.[8] Although what the symbol means is at hand in its sensuous configuration, that sensuous configuration is not limited to that meaning, but contains it among other features. For example, an image of a lion may be a symbol of courage or of kingship insofar as the lion may be characterized by being courageous and an unchallenged predator. Still, the lion possesses other attributes as well, which the symbol presumably does not express.

However, because the symbol simply presents an image, one of whose features signifies the universal quality that the symbol as a whole expresses, the symbol is not entirely adequate to the meaning it conveys. It may overcome the indifference of sense and meaning of the sign in general, but the symbol still contains a plurality of characteristics that are not all reducible to the significance it symbolizes. Moreover, these different features are all given as coeval aspects of the symbol's appearance, without any serving to identify which among the many attributes is the one privileged to convey the symbolized meaning.

Similarly, the one feature of the symbol that shares the meaning expressed by the symbol may equally comprise but one feature of the entity that the symbol represents. A king, for instance, may be symbolized by the emblem of a lion, but the king possesses innumerable other attributes besides that of being an unchallenged ruler.

Furthermore, the universal feature that the symbol conveys is not something exclusively wedded to the appearance of that symbol. Courage, for example, is not unique to lions, let alone to the particular image of a lion that may serve to symbolize that attribute.

On all these accounts, the content expressed by the symbol remains indifferent to the configuration that portrays it, despite the connection that does exist between one quality of the symbol's shape and one feature of what it conveys. Consequently, the symbol, taken by itself, is inherently fraught with ambiguity.[9]

This ambiguity confronts the audience of a symbol with three dimensions of doubt that cannot be removed by appeal to the mere appearance of the symbol. In the first place, the configuration of the symbol does not independently dictate that it be taken as a symbol, rather than as a literal representation, a sign with an arbitrary connection to its meaning, or as an "abstract" image presenting nothing but itself. Consequently, doubt can always be raised at the appearance of a symbol as to whether it should be interpreted as playing a symbolic role.[10]

Of course, such doubt can be removed by the addition and due recognition of encompassing conventions that mark out a certain configuration as a symbol. Yet, even once these conventions are at hand and adequately recognized, a second level of doubt immediately arises concerning what the symbol signifies. As a symbol, the configuration expresses a meaning linked to one or more, but not all of its features. Taking the configuration as a symbol does not of itself identify which of its features bears the meaning it symbolizes. This residual indeterminacy can be overcome in various ways, but only at the expense of destroying the relation of meaning and configuration generic to the symbol. For example, one feature of the image can be singled out through extraneous qualifications, such as in a simile, where a general idea is explicitly linked to a concrete image. That, however, renders the image merely an exemplification, rather than a symbol.[11] Similarly, the ambiguity can be removed by following a customary practice in which a certain image is habitually linked with a specific feature it bears. Since, however, it is the customary practice, rather than the character of the feature that gives it its privileged role, the shape no longer figures symbolically, but just as a sign.[12] Alternately, if the meaning of the sensuous configuration is simply identified with its own given shape, the identity and difference underlying symbolic reference is eliminated.[13] Consequently, if an appearance is to be apprehended as a symbol, without qualifications that undercut its symbolic reference, it will beckon to its audience with a meaning that is neither antecedently clarified nor explicitly expressed by the configuration itself.[14]

How then can the symbol figure as the differentiating factor of a particular form of art? From a systematic point of view, what lies at stake is taking the determinations of artistic beauty in general and considering how they get further qualified when the meaning and configuration of art take on a symbolic relation. In order for this consideration to avoid being purely arbitrary, it must also be shown that a symbolic relation between meaning and configuration in art represents one of the fundamental forms in which the significance and shape of the work of art can be united. Once a symbolic form of art has thereby been certified, it becomes possible to take up the further issues concerning its order in conception and reality in respect to the other art forms. Hegel has offered the proposal that the features generic to the symbol fit the basic option of a form of art where the meaning is too abstract to have any adequate sensuous configuration. Is this true?

In such an option, the meaning, which consists in a fundamental self-understanding of humanity, has a universality that cannot be unambiguously linked to the individual appearance of any sensuous shape. Yet, since the configuration of the work of art must be in unity with its meaning, that abstract meaning still cannot be given in any other independent shape or antecedent conceptualization. If the abstraction of the meaning was merely that of an abstract universal form, that has multiple embodiments all equally realizing the same antecedently conceivable idea, the work would forfeit its aesthetic value and revert to a mere artifact. Despite its poverty, the meaning must resist any reduction to form and technique, and instead retain a constitutive tie to the unique configuration by which it is presented. Hence, even though the appearance of the art object is not congruent with the meaning it expresses, that meaning can have no better manifestation. Consequently, the very lack of congruence between meaning and shape must be manifest in the appearance itself. This entails that elements of the configuration are expressly indifferent to the significance they bear, while the meaning of the work has an inherent uncertainty and ineffability, reflecting how it defies any adequate unveiling in thought or sensuous appearance. In these respects, the work of art here perennially *seeks* a proper shape for its significance, to borrow again Hegel's expression.

This "seeking" does not render the work of art symbolic in the sense of being a representation pointing to an independently given meaning. Nor does it give license to the aesthetically pernicious practice of turning art appreciation into a search for some content for which the work of art is a symbol.[15] It is not the work of art that, as a whole, figures as a symbol for something else. If that were the case, the putative symbolic character of the "symbolic" form of art would contradict the individuality of artistic beauty, undermining any claim that that candidate could have as a legitimate art form and relegating it to the prehistory of fine art. Rather, what is here at hand is a relation of meaning and configuration *within* the work of art that exhibits the structure of reference generic to the symbol.

The incongruity between the appearance and meaning of the work of art, where the significance cannot be unequivocally tied to its expression yet cannot be manifest in any other way, presents the same discrepancy between image and sense characterizing the symbol. Just as a symbol expresses a meaning tied to some of its features without removing all ambiguity concerning which features are to count and which of their possible senses are relevant, so here the shape of the work of art expresses a self-understanding of humanity to which the work's appearance points by indicating its own difference to what it expresses, while equally making manifest that this meaning is only as determinable as its inadequate configuration can reveal. Accordingly, the option at hand, where the meaning of art is too abstract to be in immediate unity with its configuration, can well be characterized as a symbolic form of art, without violating the individuality of artistic beauty or any of the other features of art in general that follow from it. Consequently, although Hegel may be right in recognizing how symbolic art configures abstract meanings that are not inherently individual, and accordingly creates images that are both congruent and incongruent with their sense, he is wrong to suspect that this leaves the symbolic form only at the threshold of art.[16]

What, then, remains to be determined, is how the symbolic mode of relating meaning and configuration takes hold of the different determinations of art in general in achieving its own constitution. The conception of the symbolic form of art consists in this development, whereby the existence of beauty in the work of art, the creation of the work, and its reception now get particularized in terms of its mode of aesthetic unity. The requisite conceptual resources lie already at hand as they must to uphold categorial immanence. On the one hand, we have the symbolic mode of relating meaning and configuration, which is itself determined in virtue of what is inherent in the form and content of artistic beauty. On the other hand, we have all the aspects of art in general as they have been determined. What lies at stake is observing how these aspects undergo specific modifications in realizing the particular relation of meaning and configuration minimally defining the symbolic form of art. Since the conception of these aspects follows a sequence reflecting how they incorporate one another, their particularizations in the development of forms of art will proceed in the same order.

The Content of Symbolic Art

As we have seen, the content of artistic beauty resides in a self-understanding of humanity presented in an exemplary configuration of rational agents embroiled in activities of inherent significance. Religious and ethical affairs provide the two broad domains that art transfigures in accord with its own requirement to create fundamentally meaningful images uniting individuality and universality. How does such content get qualified when meaning and configuration are symbolically related?

Since the forms of art are determined independently of the differentiation of individual arts, the defining content of symbolic art cannot incorporate any of the features distinguishing the individual arts from one another. Conversely, although symbolic art will exhibit, in common with every artform, the content generic to art in general, whatever else differentiates the content of symbolic art from that of the other artforms will be shared by every example of symbolic art, no matter what individual art it involves.

Since the content that art imaginatively transfigures consists in divine and/or secular affairs of conduct, what symbolic art presents is determined in these two respects. How these two arenas of artistic content become modified when subjected to the symbolic mode of artistic construal must now be determined.

The Construal of the Divine in Symbolic Art

The artistic portrayal of the divine faces the challenge of bringing to exemplary configuration the relation of the infinite agency of divinity with the finite agency of rational individuals. What is endemic to the artistic construal of this relation when the divine's significance for humanity is construed as something too abstract to be adequately conveyed in any individual image? Or, given how the structure of symbolic reference coincides with such an abstract meaning in art, what happens when art's imaginative shaping produces images that can only symbolize an understanding of the divine in relation to humanity for which no more privileged manifestation is available?

What lies at stake is not simply resolving the problem basic to any artistic construal of the divine: namely, how to present the infinite in its relation to finite individuals in terms of images that, as such, are inherently individual and limited. Overcoming this challenge is not yet enough to achieve the more specific task undertaken by the symbolic mode of artistic construal. What symbolic art adds to the central challenge of fitting the divine into artistic beauty is the further difficulty of treating the divine as an infinite that does not achieve unity with the finite as it is given, yet only reveals itself in the disparity between the vehicle of its manifestation and the meaning it conveys. This means that the images employed must make manifest that their restricted unique shape presents something unrestricted and universal, which is nevertheless incongruent with this, the very manifestation from which its character must be gleaned.

How can this be achieved? A mimetic approach, producing images that imitate reality as it immediately appears, is clearly of no use at all. Providing replicas of given images can hardly present a divine transcending every sensuous reality or the corresponding tension between configuration and meaning that must make itself evident. Yet, alternately, a purely non-objectivist strategy, which creates images bearing no relation to natural appearance, is no better. Such art may convey the freedom of a subjectivity whose expressions fail to achieve any determinate hold in the world, yet it cannot present the incongruity of meaning and shape that is required. Because non-objectivist configurations express nothing but their own artistry, affirming a creativity that has retreated into subjective imagination, the relation of the divine and finite individuals is lacking, as is any element of the sublime.

Between these extremes of mimesis and non-objectivism lies an alternative path that can achieve an artistic construal in the symbolic mode by modifying given appearances so that they exhibit in themselves the sought after incongruity of meaning and configuration. This can be accomplished through images that transfigure the appearance of given entities in a way that pushes explicitly against the limits of their own nature, allowing them to convey something infinite in nothing other than their own deformation. Such distortions can take either a quantitative or qualitative form. On the one hand, given entities can be imaginatively recast with quantitative alterations, magnifying their size, age, speed, and other measurable aspects to supernatural dimensions, or multiplying elements of their figure in an unnaturally boundless profusion. Alternately, given appearances can be qualitatively altered into such unnatural configurations, be it of color, sound, powers, and so on, that their fantastic monstrosity approaches sublimity. In these ways, a divinity can be configured whose limitless character appears by forcing natural appearances to transcend their own bounds by assuming imagined forms of grotesque dimension and quality. Owing to the very incongruity of sensuous appearance and divine essence, artistic imagination here knows no bounds, subjecting given phenomena to the most capricious metamorphoses. The more arbitrary and fanciful the distortion the better, since what is to be conveyed is a sense of infinitude alien to any unique, individual manifestation, yet inexpressible in any other form. On this account, the construal of the divine is symbolic, presenting in its own limited, yet distorted physiognomy features that conflict with the meaning for which it still provides the only image.[17]

As Hegel points out, a key factor in upholding the discrepancy between the sensuous configuration and abstract meaning of the symbolically construed divine is the employment of shapes that are not those in which rational agency comes to appear in its free individuality.[18] Whereas the limitless distortion of given appearances in general may serve to express an infinite that lies beyond the finite, the abstractness of the divine is equally sustained by restricting its portrayal to natural and supernatural entities alien to humanity, in the broad sense of finite rational agency with its autonomous personality. Insofar as rational agency alone comprises a domain exhibiting concrete universality, the divine would relinquish its abstractness if it were to be configured as a rational agent, whose individuality has not been obliterated by being rendered the indifferent vehicle of an extrinsic universal power, such as a transmigrating, undifferentiated world soul.

By the same token, if images of finite individuals are to be employed in symbolic construals of the relation of the divine to rational agency, they must appear such that the essence of their involvement with the divine is external to whatever unique identity they possess. For if the truth for humanity of the divine is too abstract to have any adequate shape, the configuration of rational agents must expressly reflect the insignificance of their own individuality within their ties to the divine. This may involve having individuals personify or become possessed by abstract powers, reducing their image to a faceless anonymity, or relegating them to play things of a grotesque and fantastic fate, for which their will is an empty cipher. Whereas the activities of the autonomous individual are significant in virtue of the meaning that the agent has given him or herself, here the significance of the self lies beyond as something only standing in relation to the self's own unique existence.[19]

Hegel takes these strictures of configuration to be constitutive of Oriental art's construal of the divine in respect to humanity.[20] Whether Hegel's interpretive judgment is correct is, however, an empirical matter for art historians and art critics to debate. What is of significance for aesthetic theory proper is the very different non-empirical conclusion that such configurations of the divine are ingredient in a particular mode of artistic construal that is an option endemic in the concept of artforms. How, where and when history has actualized such an option is a contingent matter lying beyond the scope of philosophical investigation.

The Construal of Conduct in Symbolic Art

The construal of conduct in symbolic art brings to bear a parallel depiction of the world situation, the particular collision from which action proceeds, and the character of the protagonists as manifest in their deeds. What here counts as universally important in ethical affairs are matters too abstract to be fully revealed in individual action, yet still incapable of any other articulation. Consequently, each aspect by which conduct figures as an object of artistic beauty exhibits the same tension between a configuration transcending its own limits and a meaning ever pointing beyond the vehicle of its expression.

The world condition, providing the setting for an exemplary collision of ethical concern, here becomes a free field for an artistic imagination wildly distorting given appearances to create a backdrop fit for conflicts, exploits, and characters sufficiently grotesque and fantastic to express meanings transcending any mundane experience. In particular, the world condition can be an environment governed by abstract powers that manipulate individuals independently of their individual initiatives, such that what conflicts arise are not rooted in anything unique to the protagonists. Alternately, the world condition can be one in which the soul of every agent is caught within an endless cycle of transmigration, diminishing the significance of whatever individuates one incarnation from another, and pointing to a meaning that transcends each moment of the whole, a meaning that nothing can make more manifest than struggles directed at freeing their protagonists from the very agency on which their strivings are predicated.

In line with such a world order, the particular collision fit for symbolic construal will involve clashes of universal powers using individuals as their pawns, struggles of a dimension and quality so fantastic as to be divorced from the given reality of rational agency, or ordeals in which individuals, asserting their independent ambitions, fight losing wars against the insignificance and illusory importance of their own unique selves.

Analogously, the character of the protagonists will either be absorbed by the powers that operate through them, possess exaggerated abilities and passions that point beyond the limits of rational agency, or alternately expend itself in a self-annulling odyssey where release from the strivings of conduct becomes the individual's own culmination.

The External Reality, Creation, and Reception of Symbolic Art

Given how the content of artistic beauty obtains a specific cast when meaning and configuration are symbolically wedded, the external reality of the work of art gets modified as well. Whatever be the individual medium in which the symbolic form gains existence, the resulting work of art will have an outer shape exhibiting the content of action, be it ethical and/or divine, in configurations of matching distortion and proliferation.

By the same token, the creation of the work of symbolic art will demand corresponding feats of wild imagination and technical dexterity to bring to aesthetic success the self-understanding underpinning symbolic art. Yet because the meaning of symbolic art is irreducibly elusive, as something with no clearer manifestation than the images that can only allude to it, the artist must work under the same searching puzzlement that the creation exhibits.[21] Whether the symbolic artist employs given forms of nature as enigmatic expressions of a transcendent meaning, distorts those forms to exhibit something sublime, or arbitrarily chooses images to make manifest a meaning incongruent with them, the creative process wrestles to express a meaning of which the artist can never possess complete clarity, searching for shapes that never fully conform.[22] Moreover, to the degree that the truth for humanity at whose expression the artist labors is one that transcends all individual reality, the individuality of the artist cannot coherently take center stage. Instead, the symbolic artist is always at work on something external to his or her own individuality, on something remaining foreign to the autonomy of rational agency.[23] The anonymity of the artist is thus the counterpart of the creation's artistic achievement.

The Primacy of Symbolic Art

Given the character of symbolic art in its construal of the divine and conduct, in its external reality, in its creation and in its reception, to what degree does it warrant any primacy in the order of either the conception or the actualization of the artforms?

The verdict on the conceptual primacy of the symbolic form of art can only be decided when the other artforms have been determined. Only then can it be established whether the other forms are at all incorporated in the specification of symbolic art and whether, conversely, these putatively subsequent forms presuppose the symbolic mode of artistic construal, either by including aspects of it in their own constitution or by making reference to symbolic art as an ingredient dimension of themselves. Of course, if the symbolic form does come first in the order of conception, then the very identity of these other forms cannot even be systematically evaluated until after symbolic art has ceased to be a topic, making way for them.

By contrast, the primacy of symbolic art in the order of existence might be decidable without appeal to any other artforms provided an account of the origin of art in general somehow entailed reference to the symbolic mode of artistic beauty.

Hegel suggests an argument along these lines in outlining what he distinguishes as the subjective and objective aspects of art's origin.[24] The subjective dimension of the genesis of art is alleged to issue from the type of wonder where the individual comes to reflect upon objectivity as a realm of universal significance fit for rational apprehension, but comes to be dissatisfied with simply revering nature as it is given and instead experiences the need to externalize the subjective consciousness of something of a more universal and essential stature. According to Hegel, art begins, subjectively speaking, when the immediate identification of nature with what is of absolute value loses its hold and is superseded by such a drive to create and contemplate a second nature of a more essential significance,[25] where meaning and configuration now stand distinguished in a unity mediated by artistic imagination.[26] The objective correlate of this development consists in natural objects no longer counting as the revelation of what is absolute and essential, but having that position taken over by creations of rational agency.[27] According to Hegel, these creations take the form of works of art before rational agents seek their truths in systems of philosophy to the degree that art offers a revelation of truth that is midway between an immediate submersion in nature and a complete withdrawal from sensuous objectivity to the realm of pure reason.[28]

Such an account has plausibility in view of the established features of artistic beauty. For if the work of art consists in imaginatively transfigured exemplary images providing a fundamental self-understanding of humanity, artistic beauty cannot come into existence without rational agents seeking truth in an aesthetic mode and without objects being produced with a correlative stature. Yet do these minimal prerequisites for the genesis of art have anything in particular to do with the symbolic artform?

Hegel offers the above argument as if it provided the initial boundary line for circumscribing symbolic art as it arises, before it exhausts its own development, reaching its final boundary by giving way to art proper, which Hegel here identifies with the classical form.[29] In this scheme of things the symbolic mode of artistic construal is alleged to come first in existence because it, unlike the other artforms, necessarily figures within this twofold genesis of art. Since whatever enters into the genesis of art cannot already qualify as art proper, symbolic art could still constitute one of the forms of art only if it figures not as a stage in, but as the necessary outcome of the coming to be of art. How can symbolic art play this temporally privileged role?

Let it be granted that when humanity first breaks from paying immediate homage to nature and puts its self-understanding in the shape of objective things of its own creation, without yet relying exclusively on thought, artists must struggle to make the appearance of created things suit the meaning they are to convey. Because classical art allegedly achieves this congruence, Hegel maintains that it cannot be the first artform. However, since the symbolic form remains caught with an incongruity between meaning and configuration, it fits the situation of art at the outset, where the attempt to make the appearance of objective things bearers of fundamental truth is still a challenge to be conquered.[30]

Yet why can art not begin with a shape fully congruent with its meaning and why then cannot classical art, not to mention romantic art, be just as primordial as its symbolic counterpart? The reason Hegel offers is that spiritual individuality, i.e., rational agency, the content allowing classical art to achieve a shape adequate for artistic beauty, can arise as an object of consciousness not immediately, but only after manifold developments, where its more abstract and indeterminate ingredients are antecedently given.[31] However, this could only exclude the primordiality or equiprimordiality of the classical form if the mediations permitting spiritual individuality to become construable arose wholly within art. If, on the contrary, such mediating developments occurred outside of art, as part of its prehistory, then the classical form could still be coeval with the advent of art. Since Hegel himself admits that rational agency becomes an object of awareness in the recognition process of self-consciousness, in every one of the structures of right comprising the institutions of freedom, and in religious representation and philosophical thought, he would need to argue that all of these prosaic phenomena are preceded by the development of art. Yet how art could arise independently of self-consciousness, let alone apart from these other prosaic realities, is hard to imagine given the very content of artistic beauty and what is inherent in its production and reception.

Nor is Hegel's analogy between the task of art at its inception and the discrepancy within symbolic construal any more of a convincing guarantor of the primordiality of symbolic art. Even if becoming an artist involves struggling to achieve the unity of shape and meaning inherent in beauty, this does not of itself condemn prospective artists to labor at symbolic construals before proceeding to classical or romantic efforts. Such a struggle is something generic to artistic production, whatever be its particular form, locality, or epoch. Consequently, the symbolic form of art cannot claim temporal primacy on this ground, even if the domain of symbolic art consists in all the modes whereby artists struggle ***towards*** giving congruent shape to the true contents of humane self-understanding, without yet achieving a proper compatibility.[32]

The Differentiation of Types of Symbolic Art

Although the genesis of art does not single out the symbolic form for a privileged baptism, Hegel still could be correct in identifying the classical form as the limiting boundary for any further developments of symbolic art. If the symbolic form is defined by an incongruity of meaning and shape, where the significance conveyed is too abstract to match any sensible configuration, whereas the classical form overcomes such discrepancy, then indeed, the classical congruity of truth and configuration can stand as an ideal towards which every type of symbolic art could be ordered in an ever narrowing approximation, which, once attained, spells the dissolution of the symbolic form and its metamorphosis into something classical.

Hegel plots the possible varieties of symbolic art in terms of just such a progression. In itself, this strategy has plausibility, since if the stages in this development can be ordered in terms of some conceptual principle, the limit of the classical form will allow the ensuing differentiation of types of symbolic art to possess an exhaustive character. This exhaustiveness would be purely conceptual, for all it would signify would be that the symbolic mode of artistic construal has a certain plurality of possible varieties. By itself, such an ordering would not carry with it any historical ramifications, such as that the history of art need actualize all of these possible varieties, let alone do so in the order in which they are conceptually determined. However, Hegel tends to imply that the conceptual ordering is an historical ordering as well, partly because he describes the types of symbolic art in conjunction with an art-critical interpretation of the historical cases that he thinks exemplify them, and partly because he develops the varieties in language suggesting a temporal and not just a logical sequence.

Consequently, if Hegel's account is taken as a resource for rethinking the possible varieties of symbolic artistic construal, two basic issues must be addressed: first, are the types that Hegel identifies properly and exhaustively defined, and secondly, is their conceptual ordering of any historical significance?

Given the demands of categorial immanence, if the differentiation of types of symbolic art is to have any conceptual necessity, it must be rooted in the determination of the symbolic form of art itself. Hegel attempts to distinguish the different kinds of symbolic art in just such a way, maintaining that they are nothing other than the possible phases and modes of the abiding contradiction that defines symbolic art.[33] This contradiction consists, as we have seen, in a joining of meaning and configuration where neither are compatible, yet where the meaning has no more adequate expression. If what is truly significant for rational agency resides in the reality of self-determination, which is concretely and not simply abstractly universal, then Hegel is correct in arguing that the discrepancy with which the symbolic form grapples is due to its embrace of an invalidly abstract content as the essence of humanity.[34] So long as art upholds such an untrue conception of what is of human significance, a conception from which individuality is lacking, it cannot possibly come up with a configuration that matches its meaning, when the sensuous appearance of the art work is irreducibly concrete. Yet does the resulting tension have a diversity of forms that can be typed by reason?

Hegel claims that the symbolic mode has three fundamental varieties and that these follow one another in a necessary order rendering them constitutive stages in the development of symbolic art.[35] Yet besides conflating a conceptual with a historical development, he injects further ambiguity much as he had done in portraying the symbolic form in general as both first mode of art and as forerunner of art proper. For in now delineating the alleged stages of symbolic art, Hegel characterizes the first as neither genuinely symbolic nor genuinely artistic, identifies the second with the transition to symbolic construal, and treats the third as symbolic art proper.[36] As a result, his typology of symbolic artforms risks turning into a differentiation of symbolic art in general from two of its antecedents.

The first stage, which Hegel labels the "unconsciously symbolic" phase, incorporates the incompatibility of meaning and shape generic to symbolic art, but does so such that this discrepancy is not itself explicit. The incompatibility is present in its minimal form in that, on the one hand, the meaning is completely abstract, signifying something of ultimate importance to humanity, but devoid of any concrete, individuating content, whereas, on the other hand, a configuration is employed that is merely natural, in the sense of being wholly external sensuous appearance lacking the inwardness of free agency.[37] These components are immediately linked together in the work of art, so that the universal significance of what is meant and its configuration are equally opaque to interpretation in terms of any distinct, mediating, elucidating content. Artistic construal here thus involves a direct identity between shape and import that remains enigmatic insofar as neither aspect contains anything specifically tying it to the other. Consequently, the configuration does not figure expressly as a symbol, offering definite attributes as possible foci of meaning.[38] Neither shape nor significance contains any feature unambiguously identifiable as the essential property determining the other.[39] Instead they present a puzzle, where the work of art possesses a configuration whose identity as a sensuous thing devoid of any essential humanizing character leaves it playing a role just as mysterious as the undifferentiated abstraction it putatively conveys. As art, what is to be expressed is of ultimate significance for rational agency. Yet the exemplary image that here should bear such meaning conveys no more than that wholly abstract ambition, doing so without any mediating grounds that would connect it with a thereby clarified truth.

Does such a mode of imaginative construal rank as a stage of symbolic art, let alone, of art in general, or is it, as Hegel equally maintains, neither genuinely symbolic nor worthy of art, but only the way station to both?[40] Or, to put the question differently, how can a mode of configuration involve symbolism that is unconsciously advanced?

According to Hegel's own self-understanding, this first stage in the development of symbolic art should exhibit the unresolved striving for congruity of meaning and shape that is generic to the symbolic form of art. Whatever distinguishes it from the other varieties of symbolic art must thus lie in the specific way in which it pursues this striving. As we have seen, unconscious symbolism is defined in terms of an immediate unity of configuration and meaning where the sensuous singularity of the former and the abstractness of the latter give their union an enigmatic character. This unity of shape and significance may formally comply with the concrete universality of artistic beauty, but the mystery of the linkage falls short of the truth that gives art its independence, *unless* it carries with it the recognition that the enigma concerns what is of fundamental importance to humanity. Provided this intimation is present, an intimation that Hegel does acknowledge,[41] the generic contradiction of the symbolic form makes its appearance. For although shape and meaning are not distinguished such that the shape conveys something both equal and different to itself, as a lion might symbolize royalty, the configuration still points to a significance that is not simply the appearance of the shape, yet is without any further definition other than that it furnish a fundamental self-understanding to humanity.[42]

In this respect, "unconscious symbolism" in art can qualify as art, and more specifically, as a type of symbolic art. Moreover, it could be said to represent the minimal form of symbolic art since it presents a disparity of meaning and shape without adding any further qualification to how the configuration and its significance are both joined and incongruent. Far from building the road to either art in general or its symbolic form, "unconscious symbolism" rather falls within art's particular realizations, giving independent shape to a dimension of artistic construal that every other form of symbolic art will incorporate with additional modifications.

This is evident in what Hegel characterizes as the second, middle stage of symbolic art: the art of the sublime.[43] In contrast to art of unconscious symbolism, which identified shape and significance without clarifying what about them joins them together, sublime art presents meaning and configuration in a negative relation, where the meaning is explicitly external to its shape without, however, having any other sensuous expression. The configuration of the work of sublime art expresses its meaning precisely by making known its own deficiency, while still providing the only shape for the truth it thereby conveys. Artistic beauty here warrants the label "sublime" because what the work of art conveys is an abstract meaning of ultimate significance transcending and nullifying its own sensuous expression. The implicit conflict of meaning and shape, which "unconscious symbolism" presented through the enigma of an art work whose purely natural configuration exhibited no determinate tie to its abstract significance, is here "consciously" at hand in imaginative images that point to an absolute meaning beyond themselves by highlighting their own limitations.[44]

Consequently, the art of the sublime incorporates the basic structure of "unconscious symbolism," where the meaning of art is conveyed by a shape that is not identical to it. However, whereas "unconscious symbolism" presents this incongruence without any clarifying ground, sublime art adds the qualification that the incompatibility of shape and meaning be mediated by a negative relation of the configuration to its own content. This content is no longer enigmatic, but rather involves familiar sensuous forms that are transfigured so as to transgress their "natural," independently given character.[45] Through such self-transgression of the shape, the meaning can therein express itself as something superseding the very entity by which it alone appears.[46] This can occur in either a positive or a negative manner, depending upon how this supersession is construed.[47] In what Hegel calls the art of sublime pantheism, the abstract, but absolute meaning is regarded as positively omnipresent in phenomena, leaving them in a self-abandoning immersion in what is of fundamental significance. Alternately, the absolute meaning can be in a negative relation to phenomena, where these manifest their inadequacy not by canceling their individuality to unite with an omnipresent substance, but by riotously violating their own natural limits.[48]

Either way, the meaning in question offers a self-understanding of humanity, construing what is fundamental to rational agency in terms of an abstract universality devoid of sufficient individuality to appear adequately in any sensible appearance, or for that matter, to do honor to the autonomy of rational agency. Accordingly, the artistic struggle to reconcile meaning and shape in the mode of symbolic art comprises an unresolved effort to inform given sensible appearances with spiritual, that is, humane significance and to render perceivable the universal dimension conceived to be essential to humanity.[49] In the art of the sublime this unresolved endeavor involves either a self-annulment of phenomenal appearance as an anonymous vessel of an omnipresent universal substance or an exaggeration and distortion of natural forms to a quantitative or qualitative monstrosity, whose boundless surpassing of mundane capacities invokes the sublime in which humanity here seeks its truth.[50] Whereas "unconscious symbolism" could present its artistic enigmas without violating the shapes of given appearance, here the art of the sublime conjures images in which artistic imagination takes natural things and occurrences and shows them immersed in an all-pervading essence indifferent to their individuality or expands them beyond all proportion to a complementary effect.[51]

Although this account of the "second stage" of symbolic art seems to match the generic features of symbolic construal, Hegel describes it as the way station to the artistic standpoint of the symbol proper, where the symbolic form achieves its consummate determination.[52] As with Hegel's similarly ambiguous categorization of "unconscious symbolism," it must be determined whether this putative stage is a bonafide type of symbolic art or a deficient forerunner relegated to the prehistory of art. Moreover, if Hegel's third alleged stage deserves its placement as the final variety of symbolic art, it must be decided whether the succession of the three types has any historical, let alone conceptual necessity.[53]

Since sublime art already exhibits the incongruence of shape and meaning basic to symbolic art, any doubts regarding its status can best be removed by examining the shortcomings that allegedly afflict it in contrast to the third stage. In terms of Hegel's account, this third stage plays a dual role of its own. On the one hand, it brings to an exhaustive completion the possible permutations of symbolic construal, incorporating the achievements of "unconscious symbolism" and sublime art, while adding the final options that symbolic art can pursue. On the other hand, this third stage brings symbolic art to an end by immanently undermining the very tension on which this artform rests.

Hegel characterizes symbolic art's third and final variety as a conscious symbolism of comparison. In virtue of sublime art's explicit presentation of the incompatibility of meaning and shape, symbolic construal is enabled to consciously separate the meaning conveyed from its artistically associated image. Sublime art makes this possible allegedly because before sensible entities can figure as exemplifications of a universal meaning to which they stand compared as factors that are related yet distinct, the given character of phenomena must be deprived of substantial worth by being relegated to an inherently null bearer of absolute meaning.[54] Otherwise, the appearances will not illustrate a separate meaning of fundamental significance, but show themselves instead. With sublime art establishing the appearances as explicitly inadequate to the meaning they convey, their meaning is implicitly severed from them and rendered independent.[55] Accordingly, sublime art has paved the way for artistic imagination to relate shape to significance as terms of a comparison where the universal content of the meaning is given independently of the configuration, which merely serves as its illustration.[56] Since the image plays its illustrative role in virtue of the external connection with its meaning, it need neither retain the appearance of given nature and convention nor undergo a fantastic expansion into the sublime. The configuration instead presents itself as a symbol produced by art, manifesting at one and the same time its own particular visage, whatever it may be, and the universal significance to which it has been correlated. It does so, somehow making evident that its connection with its meaning resides not in any essential kinship between its content and the objective features of the configuration, but in the subjective arbitrariness of the artist.[57] In this way, the art of conscious symbolic comparison preserves the ambiguity of symbolic construal, confronting its audience with the problem of imaginatively unlocking the meaning lurking within.[58]

Yet, the capricious, subjective character of the kinship of shape and meaning in comparative art, and the corresponding independent givenness ascribed the meaning that the configuration putatively illustrates, seems to reinstate the mimetic paradigm of embodied form, destroying the concrete universality, the exemplary individuality, and the unity of form and content central to artistic beauty. Just as in technique, the form is antecedently given while the matter that will receive it independently exists, so in comparative art the meaning seems to be defined apart from any outer shape, leaving its artistic expression an entirely external, arbitrary sequel, whose unique appearance adds nothing to the perfection of its illustration of the meaning.[59] This suspicion appears to be born out when Hegel develops his third stage of symbolic art as a succession of fables, parables, puzzles, allegories, metaphors, similes, didactic and descriptive poetry, and epigrams—all comprising rather dubious examples of fine art, that he himself admits are at best of a subordinate mettle.[60] Moreover, when Hegel discusses examples of these varieties of comparative art, he often chooses literary works that he elsewhere describes as classical or romantic, as if transgressing his earlier edict to address symbolic construal not as a subordinate component, but as a determining principle of artistic creation. If each of these forms simply embellishes an independently given meaning, then, indeed, the linkage of shape and significance in the comparative stage brings symbolic art to an end. For whatever wedding of form and content remains in the ambiguous identity and difference of symbolic construal would have given way to a purely external linkage alien to art.[61] And in this light, sublime art can hardly be labeled a preparation for proper symbolic construal in art, when what it introduces cannot sustain the unity of artistic beauty.

Is the comparative stage, as Hegel describes it, a retreat to that very extraneous connection of shape and meaning whose metaphorical, allegorical working Hegel otherwise condemns as a violation of every dimension of aesthetic value? With shape and meaning cleaved, with neither one any longer containing an inner affinity with the other, can comparative art still meet the requirement of symbolic construal that the difference between configuration and significance be simultaneously breached by a connection that renders the configuration the only vehicle for expressing its incompatible meaning? The link is there in the comparison the work invokes, a comparison that occurs in the awareness of artist and audience, who search for indirect similarities allowing the configuration to serve as an illustration of its meaning.[62] Although image and meaning thereby stand in contrast rather than in correspondence, their independence from one another is only relative, for neither is given apart from the relation of comparison into which the comparative artistic construal sets them. The configuration may merely illustrate what it conveys, but the meaning it expresses is not already given outside the comparison that the work elicits. In this way, the separation of shape and significance escapes the formality of embodied form and remains sufficiently tied to the individual existence of the work to fit the unity of artistic beauty, as well as the dual identity and difference of symbolic form.[63]

Nevertheless, it is debatable whether this remains true of all three of the types of comparative construal that Hegel describes. These three are distinguished according to the relative weight that each term has within the contrast of meaning and shape.

The first variety, where the contrast of shape and meaning is only implicit and the individual appearance predominates over the universal meaning that it illustrates, presents no particular problems. Fables and parables may well embrace this mode of representation, as Hegel maintains,[64] and do so without forfeiting an artistic affinity between configuration and meaning, provided their meaning does not operate as an abstract lesson that can fully resonate without the images that illuminate it.

The case is less clear in the second type, where the shape is explicitly subordinated to the universal meaning, as, Hegel suggests, in arts of allegory, metaphor, and simile. Because here the explanatory configuration can be completely capriciously chosen, the tie between meaning and shape seems utterly ruptured. Yet again, even if the connection is made through the arbitrariness of artistic imagination, it still may be possible for meaning to depend upon this individual connection for its identity.

However, any such remnant of the symbolic coupling of configuration and meaning seems lacking in the third type. Here, Hegel claims, a complete severance has been achieved, either, as in didactic poetry, by the shape of the art work becoming entirely external to the content it expresses while this universal content is already fully known in prosaic terms, or alternately, as in a rotely descriptive poetry, by the configuration having its externality presented as such, apart from any indwelling meaning.[65]

Hegel offers these correlative developments as if they brought the symbolic form to the point of eliminating itself and ushering in a new mode of unifying meaning and shape. Yet it is equally questionable whether such didactic and descriptive "arts" have any connection to symbolic construal or to the classical form that they are supposed to introduce.[66] Whereas purely descriptive construal offers a configuration devoid of any meaning for the self-understanding of humanity, its didactic counterpart offers a lesson whose "artistic" expression is entirely redundant to a prosaic teaching.[67] In each case, the separation of meaning and shape is so complete that the incongruous affinity of symbolic construal is absent. By the same token, the adequation of meaning and shape achieved in the classical form remains at a complete remove from either outcome. Indeed, the unity of artistic beauty is nowhere to be found, since didactic construal offers a message with no necessary connection to its individual expression, whereas descriptive construal presents a configuration in all its ordinary facticity with complete indifference to any universal significance lurking within.[68]

Hegel does offer one last candidate of comparative art to bridge the complementary one-sidedness of didactic and descriptive art: the epigram. Whereas didactic art leaves its universal message in a merely incidental connection to the individual configuration that delivers it, and descriptive art presents the unadorned appearance of things with no concern for any deeper meaning, the epigram allegedly inscribes its meaning onto the external thing it explains, connecting the two at the same time that they remain distinguished.[69] Nevertheless, even here, the connection between inscription and its referent remains external, since what the epigram explains exists apart in all its prior prosaic reality. Consequently, the congruent unification of the classical form remains just as remote as ever.

Yet given the antecedent existence of the phenomena whose meaning the epigram unravels, can the epigram qualify as a mode of symbolic construal, let alone as art in general? It could not qualify on either score if the epigram consisted solely in the enunciation of an abstract meaning whose sole expression consisted in the given reality of a prosaic entity. The epigram, however, consists in an original statement explaining the meaning of some phenomena, where the statement itself comprises at least one side of the expression. Consequently, the meaning is not given wholly independently of its configuration, although it does refer to some distinct prosaic reality. Whether this reference restricts the meaning to an abstract self-understanding of humanity and whether this meaning's expression is incompatible with it in the manner specific to symbolic artistic construal, is far from clear.

The Completeness of the Varieties of Symbolic Art

Granted the dubious character of certain elements of Hegel's account of comparative art, does the differentiation of unconscious symbolism, conscious symbolism, and comparative construal exhaust the alternative varieties of the symbolic form of art? Schematically speaking, these three varieties join an abstract conception of humanity with an incompatible configuration either

(1) in an immediate identity (unconscious symbolism),
(2) in a negatively mediated identity (sublime art), or
(3) in a union that is subjectively mediated by the caprice of artistic creation (comparative art).

Besides these three alternatives, one might be tempted to introduce a fourth variety, where the tie between meaning and shape is mediated, but positive in character. This remaining possibility, however, is inadmissible because it would require a configuration whose own shape *is* congruent with the meaning it expresses, positively possessing just the right features that that meaning needs for its manifestation. Such an option would transcend the limits of symbolic art, eliminating the very incompatibility on which its mode of construal rests. It would not only introduce a shape positively conforming with the fundamental truths of humanity, but inject a self-understanding of humanity that was susceptible of an adequate sensuous expression, canceling the abstract universality defining, as well as limiting, the truth to which symbolic art is wedded. It would take us beyond the symbolic form and lead us to that compatibility of form and content by which classical art becomes distinguished.

Consequently, the three modes of symbolic construal cover the field, leaving artistic imagination with the choice of following in their paths or leaping beyond into other forms of art.

3

The Classical Form of Art

Preliminary Controversies in Conceiving Classical Art

Given the logical possibilities of combining meaning and configuration in artistic beauty, the classical form occupies an intermediate position between the polar extremes prospectively identifiable as the symbolic and romantic forms of art. Whereas the symbolic form expresses a self-understanding of humanity too abstractly universal to find any congruent shape, the romantic form expresses a meaning too concretely universal to be fully exhibited in any particular sensuous configurations.[1] This leaves the classical form at the juncture between these alternatives of discrepancy, at that middle point where the self-understanding of humanity is such that it can be given a sensuous shape completely adequate to its meaning.

What significance does this placement have, and to what extent does it determine what the classical form is in its own right? As in the case of the symbolic form of art, two parallel considerations lie at hand. One consideration concerns the character of the conceptual and historical ordering of the classical form. The other concerns the relation between the classical form and artistic beauty, and between the classical form and truth.

In developing the classical form as the sequel to the analysis of the symbolic form of art, Hegel suggests that this ordering corresponds to a conceptual, as well as an historical necessity. As Hegel sees it, not only are the specifications of symbolic art presupposed by the concept of classical art, but classical art cannot come to be until after symbolic art has run its course as a real cultural phenomenon. Yet, does the intermediary logical position of the classical form entail either of these implications? Can the classical form be conceived without reference to the defining features of symbolic art? And even if the concept of classical art does presuppose features of symbolic art, does this necessitate that works in classical form can be produced only after the creation of symbolic works of art? Since the answers to these questions depend upon what the classical form is, they can only be answered after its nature has first been determined.

In conjunction with making his claims of conceptual and historical order, Hegel advances dual theses concerning the ranking of classical art. On the one hand, he maintains that the classical form is the most beautiful of all because the congruence of meaning and shape that it achieves realizes most perfectly the general ideal of artistic beauty. On the other hand, Hegel contends that the self-understanding of humanity expressed by classical art can only make its perfect fit with sensuous configuration because it suffers from a deficiently particular concept of rational agency that ties given natural factors to what is of essential value. As a result, classical art cannot give expression to the full freedom from givenness constitutive of the universal dimension of rational agency. This leaves the classical form incapable of providing a true understanding of the autonomy basic to what can be of ultimate value to humanity. Hence, although classical art may be most perfect with respect to the unity of artistic beauty, it falls short with respect to the truth it conveys. Once again, the adjudication of these assertions rests upon what the classical form comprises.

Given the demands of categorial immanence, the classical form of art can only be developed by applying its defining mode of unifying meaning and shape to the remaining features of art in general. As in the case of the symbolic form, these features get qualified in terms of the particular mode of artistic construal following the order in which they themselves have their determination. Accordingly, the content and configuration of classical art first come into play, followed by the external reality, the creation, and the reception of the classical work of art, each of which successively incorporates the features preceding its own conception. Only once these generic aspects of classical art are determined, can any internal development of particular kinds of classical art be conceived. If any other order were followed, aspects would have to be taken for granted for which no account has been given.

Solely by following this route of determination of the classical form, can the controversies concerning its conceptual and historical ordering, and its ranking with regard to beauty and truth, get resolved.

Is the Symbolic Artform the Historical and Conceptual Prerequisite of Classical Art?

If the symbolic form of art were conceptually prior to the classical form, then the most basic determinations of classical art should incorporate, or refer to, features of symbolic art. Only then will the conception of the classical form necessarily follow that of its symbolic counterpart. Similarly, the symbolic form is necessarily historically prior to the classical form only if the realization of classical art presupposes the prior existence of symbolic art either by incorporating independently existing symbolic creations or by making reference to their existence.

Accordingly, the elementary specifications of the classical form should involve aspects of symbolic art if the order of their treatment is more than a subjective convenience. Thus, even though the controversies of conceptual priority are decided by the account of the classical form in its own right, how that account involves the symbolic form is just as much an internal matter.

Since Hegel's *Lectures On Aesthetics* provides the most significant attempt to determine the classical form and its relation to the other forms of art, subjecting Hegel's argument to critique avails us of the best resource to arrive at a systematic concept of the classical form.

Not surprisingly, Hegel's account of the classical form begins with an argument to show that the classical form is predicated upon the prior achievements of symbolic art. As any theorist must do who makes symbolic art conceptually or historically prior to classical art, Hegel sets out to demonstrate how the classical form cannot be conceived independently of an antecedent determination of the symbolic form. Hegel's argument has two components. One consists in an account of how symbolic art exhibits a deficiency that classical art overcomes, and the other lies in the argument that the classical form cannot achieve its perfect unity of meaning and shape without canceling the discrepancy plaguing the symbolic form. The former component underscores the conceptual priority of symbolic art to the degree that overcoming the deficiency of the symbolic form is constitutive of the classical form. However, even if the defining character of classical art can be found by superseding the generic discrepancy of symbolic art, the classical form might still be conceivable by directly specifying a congruent unity of meaning and shape, without reference to symbolic art's vain groping. If, however, the overcoming in question is an ingredient element in the classical form, symbolic art does comprise a necessary presupposition of classical art, which then can claim historical priority as well if its canceling must occur not just within the classical form as an ingredient element, but as an independent phenomenon, occurring prior to the emergence of classical art. The second element of Hegel's argument is intended to uphold this option.

How, then, does the "deficiency" of symbolic art enter into defining the classical form? As we have seen, the symbolic form left meaning and shape in a contradictory relation of allusive affinity, where significance was joined with configuration, while the content to be expressed retained an abstract universality condemning the sensuous individuality of its expression to an ineliminable estrangement. Because the configuration served to express a meaning foreign to it, it lacked the independence of a shape that could signify itself and, in so doing, provide a fundamental self-understanding of humanity. By the same token, because the meaning could only manifest itself in a shape that was not freely expressive, it lacked the character of a significance whose essence involves giving itself an individual existence that is self-signifying, drawing ultimate meaning from its own free development, instead of personifying something else. According to Hegel, these dual deficiencies give the classical form its mandate, since so long as they persist, meaning and shape cannot achieve congruence. By the very way in which they obstruct the path to a perfected artistic unity, these emblems of symbolic art charge the classical form to convey an unconditioned meaning that entails its own individuation, and to find a shape that gives free expression to such significance.[2]

The limits of symbolic art thus mandate a dual liberation, already foreshadowed in the strivings of sublime art to raise its meaning above every sensuous given and in the effort of comparative art to render shape and significance so independent of one another that only a subjective comparison keeps them related.[3] On the one hand, the meaning of art must be freed of the immediate givenness characterizing natural existence in contrast to the mediated reality of freedom that rational agency creates for itself in exercising its autonomy. So long as what art expresses remains defined in natural terms, where factors given independently of rational agency determine what counts as fundamental to humanity, meaning will exhibit the structure of natural entities, which are always tainted by a degree of abstract universality, rather than exhibiting the concrete universality that rational agency alone brings to realization. Consequently, art will be unable to find a fully congruent, sensuous configuration for its meaning until such natural factors are excluded from what is understood to be of fundamental value.

On the other hand, the configuration employed to express artistic meaning must be simultaneously freed of shapes that are foreign to the embodiment of rational agency, as it is engaged in the free endeavors commanding inherent worth. Once such activities of individual agents are recognized to have an unconditioned value, apart from personifying transcendent powers, art is compelled to find a corresponding configuration, one that casts off the natural shapes and extensions of fantasy that must point beyond themselves to express a fundamental meaning.

These negative prescriptions do fit the generic character of artistic beauty and the basic requirement of an artform in which meaning and shape are fully congruent. Nonetheless, in and of themselves, they hardly dictate that their positive fulfillment presupposes either the concept or the antecedent reality of symbolic art.

Hegel supplies little that convincingly supports these further implications. Of least help is his argument that classical art requires a perfecting of artistic technique that presupposes the complete development of craftsmanship achieved in symbolic art's production of fixed natural shapes and of wild grotesque images.[4] Although admittedly classical art can successfully proceed only when limitations in mechanical skill no longer impede the free elaboration of form, this achievement is hardly unique to symbolic art, nor uniquely presupposed by classical art. All art requires technical mastery to give artistic imagination free play. Certainly, each artform can engender configurations of varying degrees of technical difficulty, with the purely formal creative efforts of "found" or "aleatory" art involving the minimum of mechanical skill. Yet, nothing in the differentiation of artforms guarantees any global ranking to be made of their technical accomplishment.[5] Although one might be tempted to give a special place at the bottom to romantic art in virtue of its capacity to employ completely mundane things for very unprosaic minimalisms, romantic art's alternate penchant to appropriate the other artforms for its own purposes challenges it to any technical wizardry of which they are capable.

How else then can Hegel buttress his claim that the classical artform, unlike the symbolic, cannot serve as the beginning of art, as something undertaken without other artistic preliminaries, but can only be pursued as the result of an antecedent artistic development in which the symbolic form runs its course? Hegel identifies the chief point on which this ordering is founded as the above-described focusing of content into a self-conscious individuality, clearly aware of its own essential significance, and the corollary purging of any inorganic or animal shapes, or of any human forms that are compounded with inhuman features, or emptied of their independent individuality to personify transcendent abstractions.[6]

But why can the result of this dual development not be created from scratch, without these antecedents? Hegel draws an analogy with the realization of freedom.[7] Although freedom is what it is in virtue of what it has determined itself to be, its determination cannot be an act ex nihilo. Such an act would, after all, presuppose a determiner that posits a new derivative content adding nothing to the agency of its creator, which figures as something given, rather than self-determined. By contrast, freedom, as self-determining agency, cannot already have its autonomous character at the outset, but must arrive at it as the product of its own self-constitution. Hence, free agency arises from given conditions that provide its prerequisites. Yet, in order to move from them to its self-determined reality, free agency must overcome the externality of its preconditions by incorporating them within its own domain, as components now mediated by its own self-determining process. Aristotle describes something similar in Book I of the *Politics*, recounting how the state arises from pre-political associations that then lose their antecedent, independent character by becoming incorporated within the state, which now determines what their character shall be through the activity of its own political rule. In the same way, Hegel suggests, the determination of the classical form consists in a development in which classical art engenders itself out of itself, bringing into its own sphere the presuppositions of its origin, presuppositions whose overcoming gives the classical form its own proper content and shape.[8]

That the general logic of self-determination underlies the entire categorial development of art has already been exhibited in how each successive aesthetic factor incorporates its predecessor as an ingredient factor, just as the entire dimension of art in general is first conceived apart from the particular artforms only to enter into their determination as components now mediated by their governing mode of artistic construal. Yet to describe the turn from symbolic art to classical art as a succession of this sort simply begs the question, unless it is substantiated by showing *how* classical art both constitutively incorporates the symbolic style and originates from its generic discrepancy of meaning and configuration.

The proof of the pudding lies in the constitution of the classical artform itself. So far, the only avenue of support left to Hegel's dual theses of conceptual and historical ordering is his yet to be adjudicated claim that the classical style's transformation of meaning and configuration can only occur as the result of a double disenchantment of nature removing essential human significance from both nature's general inorganic powers, and plant and animal life.[9] By undercutting the artistic rationale for personifying natural powers or investing inhuman organisms with symbolic meaning and shape,[10] this achievement certainly clears the way for making rational agency the true content for art and the appearance of humanity the true form for giving that meaning a congruent expression. Yet, whether this double overcoming of symbolic style is necessary for the genesis and/or ingredient in the actuality of classical art can be decided only by an examination of the classical style itself.

The Meaning and Shape of the Classical Form

The minimal characterization of the classical form involves more than simply the congruence of meaning and shape. Although the logical possibilities of combining meaning and configuration in artistic beauty could be abstractly stated in terms of two polar types of discrepancy and one compatible union, each option gains further dimensions when the specific content of artistic beauty is taken into account.

As we have seen, in order for symbolic art to present a configuration that could only allude to a meaning too abstract to have any adequate sensuous expression, natural determinations played a preeminent role in defining both the content ascribed to the essence of humanity and the forms of its appearance. As a consequence, the configurations of symbolic beauty were marked by a dependence. They always signified a meaning residing not in their own individuality, but in some foreign element, just as their truth for humanity always resided in something transcending the independent autonomy of individuals.[11]

By the same token, when classical art achieves a congruity of meaning and shape, the meaning and shape involved have just as specific a content as the truth they provide. Because meaning and shape are here perfectly at home with one another, artistic configuration expresses a meaning clearly and unambiguously resident within it,[12] whereas artistic meaning comprises a self-understanding of humanity that individuates itself into just such a shape. As a consequence, neither side is dependent upon anything else for its aesthetic substance. Each element rather exhibits a free independence that at the same time joins them together.[13]

Because natural determination, left in its immediate givenness, is neither independently meaningful nor a vessel that can adequately express the self-determining creation of meaning characterizing rational agency, the independence of the classical style requires a different focal point. What alone can bring congruity to meaning and shape, affording a self-signifying configuration and a meaning that entails an individual sensuous appearance is the phenomenon of rational agency itself,[14] provided it be engaged in affirming the essential significance of its own freedom, yet doing so such that what counts as essential in its endeavors is precisely what appears to sense. If art takes as the focal point of imaginative construal the configuration of rational agency as it appears in free action, generating a second nature expressing its autonomy,[15] this shape will perfectly express a self-understanding of humanity that rests ultimate value in the outer manifestation of conduct. Classical art then will make its privileged form the sensuous figure of rational agency as it exhibits such conduct, a figure bearing its own individual character as central to its significance, a figure thus shorn of any vestiges of extraneous inhuman, animal distortions, or of transcendent personifications.

Yet, because such a figure must be fully significant in how it appears, it will not exhibit a character whose essence resides in a hidden inwardness, where conscience reigns, disputing the all-importance of the outward appearance of action, and where inner struggles of subjective faith take precedence over public deed. Consequently, whereas the figure of rational agency must be liberated of vestiges of inhuman content, it must exhibit a character whose worth resides exclusively in how it outwardly appears, lacking the dimension of an essential interiority, which permits autonomy to rise beyond the immediate givenness of outer appearance. Only then will the sensuous figure of rational individuals adequately express what is worthy in humanity and only then will the essence of humanity be positively construable in a particular shape. Under these conditions, the existence of rational agency can reside no where else than in its bodily appearance, which itself counts as nothing but the expression of its animating spirit.[16]

Accordingly, the given appearance of rational agency must undergo a twofold idealization to become an appropriate shape for classical art. First, any residual natural features that remain inexpressive of and incidental to rational agency must be expunged.[17] This involves purging from view those aspects of the body and its activity that are purely natural, such as all those features and functions that may be essential to animal existence, but contribute nothing significant to the strivings of rational agency, as well as any other manifestations that reflect influences and contingencies extraneous to humanity.[18] Second, any visible trace of a cherished inwardness detaching the worth of individuals from the outer appearance of their activity must be stricken. This involves restricting the show of character to an individuality imbedded in an ethic of community, caught up in struggles between the public demands of different ethical spheres, yet free of any separate inner turmoil of personal conscience.[19] In each respect, the appearance of rational agency must be transfigured to make its figure perfectly express the humane significance of its outer life. Needless to say, this applies to not only the physical attributes on display, but also the emotions, desires, and activities that are concomitantly on view.[20]

Hegel's Suspect Limitations upon the Classical Form

Hegel duly identifies the basic dimensions of this concretion of the classical form, yet in doing so he attaches three claims of a suspect narrowness:

(1) that the human figure provides classical art's privileged configuration,[21]
(2) that classical art incorporates a culturally given content,[22] and
(3) that this content involves a depiction of the overcoming of the vision of humanity exhibited in symbolic art.

To begin with, is Hegel correct to conflate the figure of rational agency with the appearance of human species being and to argue, thereupon, that the classical form must make its defining configuration the human shape? Admittedly, the human figure is, of all known terrestrial appearances, the one most suited to exhibit rational agency in a sensuous embodiment. Yet, nothing in the concept of rational agency mandates that it can only take human form. Just as ethics cannot be limited to human species being, so in matters of artistic beauty, humanity can only play a constitutive role if it is understood to encompass all conceivable finite rational agents, be they homo sapiens or not. For this reason, classical art could conceivably employ figures of actual non-human rational creatures, were they to exist and artistically express themselves on extraterrestrial abodes, or use imaginatively fantasized figures that are recognizable as rational agents, unmarred by bestial features or the facelessness of a personifying cipher. Ancient Greek art's fixation upon the human figure may exemplify the classical form, but it hardly provides its rule.

Is there more legitimacy to Hegel's second claim that the transparent adequacy of meaning and shape in classical construal involves the incorporation of a preexisting content that classical art appropriates from its encompassing culture?

In support of this thesis, Hegel points to how ancient Greek art took its material from the myths of Greek religion, myths that already had a suitable character owing to their anthropomorphic polytheism.[23] Yet, the mere facts of Greek art can hardly dictate necessary features of the classical artform, since what might be true of Greek classicism could be a contingent accident of no bearing upon other realizations of the classical style. Moreover, Hegel's own account of Greek art undermines his own claims, for repeatedly he acknowledges that the myths of ancient Greek religion were first produced by Greek artists, rendering ancient paganism a religion of beauty that issues from, rather than conditions, Greek art.[24]

On a more systematic plane, Hegel suggests that classical art must draw its motifs from a preexisting cultural heritage because classical construal can only achieve its congruence of meaning and shape if it has a settled content to incorporate and transfigure. Only then, Hegel maintains, can classical artists produce configurations that go beyond the ambiguous allusions of symbolic construal, seizing upon a transparent content, already known independently of artistic creation, yet fully susceptible of artistic expression.[25]

If such were the case, classical art would come perilously close to the mimetic ideal, realizing an antecedently given content available to knowing independently of its artistic embodiment. Yet if classical art had to begin with prior knowledge of what it realizes, how could it avoid collapsing into an exercise of craft, producing artifacts whose individual appearance is indifferent to their perfection? Hegel would like to dismiss this problem by suggesting that the content in question perfectly matches its sensuous configuration, allowing every unique detail to be essential to the meaning. However, if such congruity were at hand, how could the content be known prior to the creativity of artistic imagination? Admittedly, if the content were at hand in religious, as opposed to scientific representation, it would have a figurative dimension. Yet if the images of religious narrative are to be set apart from those of art, they must contain a prosaic dimension lacking the concrete universality of beauty. If, alternately, religious imagery is fully beautiful, as Hegel intimates is the case in the "religion of beauty" of ancient Greece, the allegedly antecedent source for the content of classical art already counts as an example of classical art, which then has no antecedents of its own.

Although classical art, like any other artform, may draw upon given meanings in its own creations, it cannot simply appropriate prior contents without submitting them to the artistic transfiguration that allows them to fit the configurations specific to the classical mode.[26] Moreover, the special match of meaning and shape in classical art is not dependent upon a prior knowledge of content awaiting expression. The lucidity of the classical form is a product, rather than a presupposition, of artistic creation. Plato not withstanding, the classical artist may well achieve a clarity about the meaning of his or her creations that symbolic artists never reach. However, this understanding can be won within the process of artistic creation, as the artist gradually refines the work to the point where its appearance expresses a naturally determined rational autonomy whose sensuous manifestation reveals all its significance.

Hegel himself provides arguments in support of this very conclusion.[27] Since the content of classical art is the free individuality of rational agency that realizes its autonomy in the sensuous appearance of its bodily existence, the form conveying such independence requires a corresponding freedom. The immediate givenness of natural appearance will not do, due to all the externally determined elements that burden it with contingencies indifferent to the expression of rational agency. Instead, the link of sensuous existence and free individuality must be an artificial one, issuing from the autonomous activity of rational agency. Otherwise, the connection between form and content would be imposed upon each side, undercutting their constitutive independence. Accordingly, the classical artist creates with a dual freedom: laboring free of natural forms and personified abstractions that leave obscured the meaning of the work, and freely producing forms purifying humanity's own facticity of its natural obduracy, engendering an artificially shaped ideal in which artist and audience find a clear display of their own free being, perfectly at home in its transfigured bodily existence.

Although the resulting shape is determined by the content, this freedom precludes classical creation being limited to appropriating a cut and dried theme and shaping a congruent configuration. The development of form is not, as Hegel suggests, the overriding focal point of classical artistry,[28] but rather a perfectly matched counterpart of the working out of a suitable content that exhibits the self-understanding of classical construal. Classical creation can achieve its aims only when both sides proceed in tandem, transfiguring the natural appearance of rational agency in conjunction with transfiguring the strivings of humanity into an independent, but fully public content.

Dismissing Hegel's first claim about classical art, that it take the human form as its privileged shape, need not undermine his third assertion that classical art necessarily incorporates some depiction of the overcoming of the self-understanding generic to symbolic art. Widening the shapes of the classical form to that of non-human rational agents still allows for portrayals of the defeat of the symbolic ideal, which can itself incorporate such agents for its own fanciful and personifying uses. However, repudiating his second claim that classical art must incorporate an antecedently given content, might appear to bar any introduction of symbolic motifs since these, even when presented in the act of being overcome, would still possess a prior character. Nonetheless, classical art's liberation from bondage to prior givens does not preclude the incorporation of such contents; it only removes their mandatory presence and dictates that when they are included, their own meaning becomes transfigured within the new imaginative context in which the classical artist places them. Accordingly, classical art could well depict the overcoming of symbolic ideals provided they receive the subordinate treatment conforming to the self-understanding of the classical style, such as in ancient Greek portrayals of the defeat of the old deities of natural forces by the new anthropomorphic gods.

Still, permitting this option is one thing, mandating it as necessarily ingredient in classical art is another. If classical artists can just as well create new legends as incorporate the old to achieve congruence in meaning and shape, why can they not give the natural shape of rational agency an independent meaning with or without tying it to the annulment of symbolic ideals? What alone could require that tie would be an inability of the natural appearance of humanity to exhibit an autonomous worth, without appearing as the result of a striving depriving nature of any sacred or supernatural value, and investing rational agency with a self-won centrality at home in the world of phenomena. Such an inability would underwrite the conceptual priority of the symbolic over the classical style and underscore the historical priority of symbolic art to the degree that art could appear in a symbolic style without need of antecedent or coeval classical art, whereas classical art would require at least the accompaniment of symbolic artistry.

Hegel argues for such a tie, not so much as a constant feature of classical art, but rather as a factor distinguishing the first stage of the classical form's own development.[29] This tie allegedly falls by the wayside once classicism leaves behind its archaic origins and appropriates the shape of rational agency for its new self-understanding. At that point, classical art can take a new avenue of development consisting in exhausting the possibilities of the congruence it has attained.

However, what distinguishes particular stages in the development of classical art are not generic features of classical art. If reference to the overcoming of the symbolic ideal is the distinguishing mark of only one kind of classicism, it cannot fall within the content constitutive of classical beauty. At best, it will represent a factor ingredient in one possible variety of classical art, which then will presuppose the symbolic artform. The other varieties of classicism will still escape any such presupposition, provided they are not predicated upon the variety in question.

Consequently, before this alleged development of varieties of classical art can be determined, the universal nature of classicism must be fully established. So far, only the most rudimentary aspects of the meaning and configuration of classical beauty have been introduced. Following the order of the categories of beauty in general, the classical form must next be elaborated in respect to the two domains of content susceptible of artistic construal: humanity in its relation to the divine, and ethical conduct.

The Classical Construal of the Divine and Conduct

Given how the classical ideal has rational agency for its content and form, with the independent value of individuals entirely manifest in their external appearance, how do the divine and conduct get configured in classical art? Because classicism affirms rational agency in its sensuous existence, with no heed paid to any concealed inner dimension, humanity is stamped with particularity, tying its essence to specific external features fit for images but opaque to the universality of thought. As Hegel points out,[30] this does not tie the shape of rational agency to one single type, for that would cancel its particularity and render it something universal. Instead, it presents a plurality of specific configurations of humanity, that is, of specific characters, each of fundamental significance, communicating a meaning that can be given no better formulation than in the exemplary figure they comprise in their immediate appearance.

Applied to the divine, the classical style engenders a pantheon of particular deities, each taking the shape of a rational agent. Since rational agency is not an anthropological fact, the divine of the classical ideal may or may not take human form. Whatever species of rational agency it embraces, the divine will be particularized into a polytheism. If the divine were confined to a monotheistic representation, it would forfeit its particularity owing to the absence of the constrastive plurality to which the particular owes its identity. In that case, the divine could no longer be entirely immersed in the particularity of the image in which it manifests itself, an immersion required of the classical ideal.

Yet, owing to its particularization into a plurality of individual characters, the divine is in peril of losing whatever infinitude still distinguishes its rational agency from that of the finite individuals to whom it provides essential significance. Although the classical deities, as divine, still preside over humanity, their plurality leaves the power of each divinity limited by one another and in the service of particular ends, rendering their interaction prey to contingencies[31] akin to a drama of finite individuals writ large. Moreover, to the degree that all are thereby subject to an external fortune comprising the common pervasive emblem of their limitations, deities and mortals alike will find themselves ruled by inescapable powers of fate.[32] If such fate were to be an individuated force in its own right, it would merely fall beside the other deities as one of their vulnerable brethren. Hence, to retain its role as the other side of the sensuous, particular identity of individuals, this fate must remain an impersonal, indeterminate necessity, to whose unpredictability all must submit.[33]

As for the classical construal of conduct, two desiderata will apply whether character and action involves divinities, mortals, or dealings among the two. Whatever their mortality, individuals will be represented as independent rational agents whose own external strivings are the focal point of ultimate meaning. Consequently, the conflicts on which exemplary action proceeds will not focus upon yearnings of the heart as they stand opposed to the outer reality of action, but rather upon clashes of deeds and of public commitments. Consequently, what stands at center stage is the pathos of conduct, with character serving the action instead of action serving as a vehicle for a development of individual personality in all its internal emotional life.[34]

Although the existence of inner turmoil need not be denied, the classical ideal mandates that the significance of conduct lies not in the moral dimension of the choice of motives or in private passions, but rather in the ethical realm where actions count by realizing goods that either are already publicly embodied in existing institutions or whose achievement by a founding hero brings such institutions into being.[35] Nevertheless, since ethical conduct is purposive, it remains subject to inner conflicts. Consequently, these struggles of the heart still come into play in the classical construal of conduct, not as independently meaningful, but in their connection to the external performance of deeds ingredient in the actuality or genesis of ethical community. Whether this focus upon the ethical to the exclusion of the moral mandates such particulars as an epic as opposed to a novelistic treatment[36] is something to be determined within the theory of artistic genres where the realization of classical beauty in the individual arts is properly at issue. However, the exclusive focus upon the ethical does signify that classicism gives artistic expression to a self-understanding in which what individuals consider essential is fully achievable within the way of the world, where, to paraphrase Lukács, outer deeds can satisfy the soul's demands for greatness, since life is fundamentally homogeneous with intrinsic value, allowing human striving to realize essential aims already at home in the closed and complete totality of public existence.[37]

The External Reality, Creation, and Reception of Classical Art

Does the unity of meaning and configuration in classical beauty entail any particular ramifications for the eternal reality of the work of art, ramifications that are given independently of the differentiation of individual artistic genres? If any further qualification applies, it simply amounts to conforming the outer being of the artwork to the centrality of the appearance of rational agency, the focus upon external ethical conduct (be it of deities or finite individuals), and the idealization of the rational figure in function of these concerns. Little else can be added without bringing into play the different media of the individual arts.

Does the classical congruence of meaning and configuration add anything more specific to artistic creation in general? If, contra Hegel, the classical artist is ***not*** bound to portray the human figure, incorporate culturally given meanings, nor depict the overcoming of symbolic ideals, what remains distinctive about the creative process of classicism? Hegel himself introduces basic distinguishing features, which, though presented in conformity with his unwarranted restriction to human species being, can be easily freed from this taint.

First, because classical art draws its content neither from natural forms nor abstract divinities alien to humanity, but rather from rational agency as it appears to sense, classical artists are in a position to give expression to what is closest to their own immediate existence.[38] Symbolic artists must struggle with fundamentally foreign configurations to give expression to a self-understanding that can only be alluded to, so that even when they employ the human figure, they are at pains to abstract away its individual selfhood to render its form the personification of powers lying beyond humanity. By contrast, classical creators are at home with themselves in their artistry, turning their energies to conjuring beauty in the appearance they share as rational agents, in expression of their own fundamental value.

Accordingly, the imaginative transfiguration of classical artists centers upon taking the given appearances of rational agents, stripping away every remnant of natural contingency and external dependency that obscures the embodiment of rational agency as engaged in actions of mortals and humanized deities that have their worth by contributing to ethical community, without regard for the inner dimension of moral subjectivity. Since, in this reworking of given appearances, classical artists forge a shape in which rational agency adequately manifests itself in its fundamental meaning, they create a work of whose significance they have no reason to be ignorant. As Hegel suggests, classical artists can therefore create with a lucid self-awareness eluding symbolic artists,[39] exercising a creativity both self-sufficient and restrained in function of the determinate character of their art's content and of how its shape completely belongs to that content.[40]

Such transparency and independence will infuse the reception of classical art, delivering its appreciation from having to unravel symbolic allusions. Once the audience recognizes a work to be classical, it will cease searching for the answers to puzzles, and cease searching for the sublime in grotesque exaggerations of natural form, cease looking for powers personified in faces whose individuality has been blanked out. Instead, attention will turn to how a configuration exhibits the independent value of a naturally determined rational agency in harmony with its sensuous appearance.

The Dissolution of Classical Art

As much as classical art may achieve a unity of meaning and shape paradigmatically realizing the concrete universality of artistic beauty, the self-understanding it provides still suffers from a limited content that prevents classicism from consummating art's revelation of truth. Classical art could be without peer in respect to this cognitive dimension of beauty only if the fundamental truths of humanity met two conditions. First, the highest values of humanity would have to be susceptible only of an exemplary embodiment, such that the measure of conduct could never be fully determined in the universal dimension of conceptual principle, but could only be found in the paragon of existing individuals and their actions. Then, the image of these exemplars would provide the most adequate rule of life, allowing classical configuration to be the last word on conduct. Second, the exemplars of value would have to be restricted to individuations of external religious and ethical conduct, rather than of inner resolves of faith and morality. Only then would the paragon be fully manifest in sensuous appearance, allowing classical art to present the whole truth and nothing but the truth.

However, freedom, which alone commands the unconditioned universality of normativity, is neither opaque to reason, nor exhaustively manifest in the spheres of ethical community. The structures of self-determination involve universal principles at every level.[41] The property relations of persons, the resolves of morally accountable subjects, the rights and duties of family members, the economic, legal and corporate bonds of civil society, and the self-governance of citizens all involve lawful conduct for whose rule no exemplar can substitute. Moreover, the reality of freedom remains incomplete if moral self-determination is excluded.[42] Consequently, if art is to provide an adequate self-understanding of what is of ultimate value to rational agents, it cannot be limited to the resources of classical construal.

Classical art has brought the individuality of rational agency into beauty in the shape of existing agents, but, as Hegel aptly observes, this shape is taken as it immediately appears, in its corporeal external manifestation.[43] Contrary to the classical self-understanding, this immediate existence is not equivalent to humanity per se, for it bars from view the inner domain of subjective consciousness and with it, the experience of humanity recognizing the fundamental importance of its inner subjective life in respect to religious faith or moral accountability.[44] To the degree that the true totality of rational agency involves this inner element in conjunction with its external counterpart, classical beauty cannot make manifest the full animation of individuals.[45] For this reason, Hegel repeatedly points to the substantial repose of classical figures,[46] be they divine or mortal, a repose reflecting both the fundamental significance of what their external appearance makes manifest and the concomitant unimportance of their inner life.[47]

Moreover, as already intimated, this seizing upon the external appearance of rational agency places the classical construal of the divine in a bind. Although configuring deities in the shape of individual rational agents overcomes the deficient abstractness and natural determination with which symbolic art shapes the divine, it subjects divinity to external contingencies and divides it into particular individuals whose unity is as arbitrary as persons in a state of nature. This leaves the deities of classical art in jeopardy of relinquishing their infinitude and reverting to demigods subject to a faceless fate in common with mere mortals. As a result, the classical style achieves its congruity of meaning and shape only at the expense of failing to convey rational agency and the divine in their totality.[48]

This shortcoming presents an incentive to overcome the classical style provided artists create in function of comprehending and remedying classicism's limitations by engaging in a new mode of artistic construal that can give rational agency its full due. Whether artists actually do take this route is a historical question that is distinct from the "logical" issues of whether a remedy is conceivable and to what degree it exhausts the basic possibilities of the forms of art. Any claim of a historical necessity impelling such a development in artistic style must confront the possibilities of artists simply remaining unaware of the limitations of classicism, being unable to come up with any further mode of artistic construal, abandoning classical art in a reversion to symbolic artistry and its self-understanding of humanity, or even becoming extinct through natural or artificial calamities.

Nonetheless, if artists do undertake a new mode of joining meaning and configuration, whether it must be preceded in reality and/or conception by the classical style will be decided by the internal character of the resulting artform. That the new artistic style overcomes the limitations of classical art does not guarantee that classical construal is the emergent style's necessary presupposition in actuality or thought. As manifest in the relation of the symbolic and classical artforms, priority is not established by the emergent artform simply incorporating another artform that can exist and be conceived independently of it. The new artform must also require the antecedent conception and/or realization of the other style. Otherwise, the two forms could still be coeval in theory and practice.

Hegel identifies the new alternative as the romantic style, claiming that it at one and the same time overcomes the limitations of classical art and exhausts the differentiation of artforms. Moreover, Hegel introduces romanticism as necessarily subsequent to classical art in both conception and reality.[49]

Yet, in laying out the transition from classicism to romanticism, Hegel maintains that the development occurs in virtue of a religious transformation external to art. Whereas, in Hegel's own account, the overcoming of symbolic art by classicism was carried out within classical art in the imaginative portrayal of the overthrow of nature gods by anthropomorphic deities, romantic art is heralded by an actual religious event, where the content of the divine gets withdrawn from the artistic figures of classical creation and invested in an actual individual, whose prosaic reality is a key element in the constitution of a new self-understanding of humanity.[50] Such an origin seems to rest the development of the artforms upon a *Deus ex machina*, rendering their succession of questionable necessity, to say the least. Nonetheless, Hegel maintains that if the transition from the Greek gods to the Christian Almighty had been made by art, the overthrow of the classical deities would remain a work of imagination that could not be taken in full earnest.[51]

To account for romantic art by appealing to an historical development external to aesthetic phenomena is just as wrongheaded as to search for a cause in the artform that allegedly precedes romanticism in conception and/or actuality. If romanticism were determined by factors extraneous to art, then its status as an artform per se would be overturned, rendering it a historical phenomena relative to a contingent fact. Moreover, conditioning the romantic form upon a religious development provides no resource for distinguishing it in its specifically aesthetic character from any other phenomena alleged to issue from that event. Each derivative entity will be in the same relation to the ground it shares in common with the rest, whereas this ground will provide no basis for deciding which phenomena will be determined by it, nor how they will be differentiated from one another. Conversely, if one artform is treated as the principle for establishing the identity of another, the "new" artform is rendered a derivative function of its predecessor, deprived of any resource for maintaining its own irreducible individuality.

By appealing to a prior ground to determine romanticism, both of these explanatory options disrupt the immanent development of systematic argument, where antecedent terms may enter in as ingredients of a subsequently conceived factor, but without determining what distinguishes the latter in its own right. If romanticism can count as an alternative to symbolic and classical artforms that resolves their difficulties while exhausting the modes of artistic construal, it may incorporate elements of these two counterparts, not as causes of its own character, but as components that take on a new significance within the new whole to which they now belong.

Accordingly, if, as Hegel suggests, one could substantiate a necessary dissolution of classical art within its own domain,[52] this breakdown would still not supply the positive principle defining a new artform. Hegel locates an alleged transition within classical art in the withdrawal of rational agency from the external appearances of public life into the private recesses of inner life as a new privileged arena of value. This withdrawal allegedly arises on two accounts inherent in the classical ideal. On the one hand, the outer world in which rational agency invests its individuality is plagued by contingency and particularity, leaving the divinity of the gods just as vulnerable to the vicissitudes of fortune as the institutions of ethical community. On the other hand, the exclusion of private individuality from any honored significance leaves the inner world of the subject in latent conflict with external convention.[53] The resulting cleavage between the inner consciousness of the individual and public life breaks the harmony to which the classical form gives expression.[54] If art is to create configurations appropriate to the self-understanding of humanity forged in this cleavage, classicism must undergo a transformation. Hegel cites the comedy of Aristophanes and Roman satire as paradigms of the resulting self-supersession of classical art, where external reality is shown being depleted of fundamental significance for rational agents, whose subjective consciousness stands in contempt of their world, comprising in that same critical relation the only remaining point of meaning.[55]

If the cleavage were complete, with all significance withdrawn from outer appearance and locked up in the intellect of individuals, the situation would be, as Hegel himself admits, a purely prosaic one,[56] with no opportunity for the unification of meaning and configuration required for beauty. However, meaning is here invested not simply in subjective awareness, but in individuals' negative relation to external reality. Because this relation is exhibited in actions unmasking the corruption of existing institutions, it seems that it can be given shape as the focal point of a transitional mode of construal.

What then would lie at hand would be an incompatibility of meaning and shape that is the opposite of the incongruence besetting symbolic art. Even in symbolic art's most extreme discrepancy between significance and configuration, where their only tie lay in their comparison, this comparison still depended upon some residue of similarity permitting the two sides to convey, rather than annul, one another. By contrast, the proposed dissolution of classical art sets the self-understanding of humanity at odds with humanity's external reality, engendering a relation of enmity rather than kinship.[57]

As Hegel underscores,[58] the opposition does not lie in a reversion to the abstractions of symbolic self-understanding. These lacked the individuality allowing subjective consciousness to retain any fundamental significance. Here, by contrast, the opposition to external existence resides in the individuality of rational agents, which has ceased to identify with outer convention and made itself in its critical independence a source of meaning. Such an individuality is free in the negative sense of liberating itself from immediate, sensuous existence and retreating into its inner life as a locus of value. What this individuality lacks is any objective realization for its autonomy. Missing this positive dimension of freedom, rational agency is only abstractly autonomous, beset with conflict with outer existence and thereby rendered a finite agency implacably limited by this unresponsive other. This, its counterpart, is a correlatively liberated world, free of any indwelling significance for rational agents, just as godless as it is alien to its inhabitants. To the degree that this world contains institutions claiming any value for themselves, these can only be corrupt impostors. As a whole, then, the new self-understanding presents the intractable opposition of a finite subjective agency and a degenerate world.[59]

In presenting satire as the transitional artform giving shape to this emergent discord of independent subjectivity and its degenerate world, Hegel leaves satire with a problematic status. On the one hand, if satire is not yet the new artform of romanticism, which putatively completes the possible options of artistic construal, do these options become a foursome, with symbolic, classical, satirical, and romantic styles on a par? Or is satire a mode of classical art, comprising the last stage in the self-dissolution of classicism? On the other hand, does satire count as a bonafide example of art any more than did didactic or descriptive poetry, which Hegel had introduced as final stages of symbolic art?

To the extent that satire revolves around the disharmony of subjectivity and the appearances of its world, Hegel maintains that it does not produce genuine artworks.[60] If this is so, satire should count neither as a stage of classical art nor as an artform in its own right. Yet, Hegel offers a disclaimer, observing that, however prosaic satire tends to be, it can command aesthetic value if it configures the world into a shape whose corruption collapses through its own senselessness.[61] The concentration of value in subjectivity then no longer remains prosaically hidden within consciousness, but makes itself manifest in outer appearances, permitting a genuinely artistic dissolution of degenerate convention.[62]

In that case, does satire fit within classical art or does it emerge as a new artform, either distinct from romanticism or comprising romantic art's own first appearance? On one account, Hegel's own response is unambiguous: satire has not attained the plateau of romanticism. Whereas satire remains bound to an inner disposition that cannot reconcile itself with the outer world and give positive determination to its autonomy, the romantic form gives shape to a self-understanding of rational agency in which individuality enjoys both an independent subjectivity and an objective actuality in a world recognizing the agent's inner worth.[63] Moreover, Hegel maintains, satire's cleavage of finite subjectivity from external objectivity represents a way station at which art cannot linger without forsaking its constitutive unity of meaning and shape.[64] Even if satiric construal can shape images of the internal dissolution of a corrupt world, satire is unable to provide any positive determination for the subjective agency it sets free from the ruins. The aesthetic worth of such images can be questioned, for they are incapable of providing a self-understanding of humanity with any affirmative content. To this degree, the art from which they issue lacks a meaning worthy of aesthetic transfiguration, let alone one susceptible of representation in an individuated sensuous appearance.

This leaves such satire an artistic no man's land, issuing from the dissolution of classical beauty, but not delivering the principle for defining romantic art. As such, satirical artistry must be left behind if the forms of art are to be consummated.

4

The Romantic Form of Art

The Aesthetic Challenge of Modernity and the Problematic of Romantic Art

With the rise and global expansion of modernity, art has increasingly become a problem. Cast adrift from the fixed bearings of traditional shape and meaning while enduring the pressures of market necessity and public subsidy, art has confronted a dilemma internal to its own aspirations, calling into question the very significance of its enterprise. Through the crucibles of the Enlightenment, the Reformation, capitalism, the American and French Revolutions, and social democracy, a world has begun to come into being recognizing no other authority than the autonomy of reason and will. The rights to property, moral accountability, a free household, equal economic opportunity, and self-government have become ever more acknowledged as universal principles revoking legitimacy from any particular factors given independently of self-determination, such as hereditary rank, race, gender, sexual orientation, or ethnicity. And through the widening struggles over erecting free households, civil societies, and political democracies, the divide between the modern and the pre-modern has been drawn by a normative agenda in which the universality of free agency is to be realized in a self-sustaining system of institutions of freedom.

This normative agenda has, of course, been challenged by postmodernism, which calls into question the autonomy of reason and conduct by unmasking the historical factors that allegedly condition what counts as true and right. Although post-modernism is equally skeptical of reverting to the pre-modern path of accepting the authority of certain privileged givens, post-modernism capitulates to the hegemony of arbitrary givens in general by denying the possibility of freeing discourse and action from the hold of rationally inscrutable contexts of convention. For this very reason, post-modernism cannot coherently advance the authority of its own characterization of the predicament of theory and practice. Either post-modernists must admit the ideological bias of their own position or they must lay claim to a neutral omniscience contradicting their own deconstructions of the conditioning factors of knowledge and value. Hence, whatever acclaim post-modernist ideology may receive, it cannot successfully overcome the project of modernity.[1]

The rise of that project has thrown art into a crisis. For if art is to rise above entertainment and edification by giving an indispensably revelatory sensuous shape to fundamental human truths, how is it to retain any significance when the self-understanding of humanity affirms the universal claims of autonomy and casts in aspersion the independent value of all external particulars? If every particular given is now incapable of providing an exemplary realization of freedom, how can art's sensuous configurations any longer lay hold of fundamental truths?

This problem may have become the order of the day with the particular historical developments giving birth to modernity, but it represents a challenge rooted in the logical possibilities of artistic construal. The peculiarly modern predicament of art embodies the difficulty confronting the aesthetic unification of meaning and configuration once the options of the symbolic and classical artforms have been supplanted by the one remaining alternative, an alternative comprising the romantic form of art.

The Deduction of Romantic Art

The determination of a third and final mode of artistic construal proceeds from two complementary considerations. One consists in the formal delineation of the possible relations between the meaning and configuration of artistic beauty, a delineation focusing simply upon how the two terms can be joined in respect to identity or difference. As we have seen, three basic options are possible: meaning and configuration can or cannot accord, and if they are incongruent, meaning may be either too abstract to fit the individuality of sensuous shape or too concrete to be limited to any particular appearance. This division becomes further qualified in light of the possible types of world view comprising the content of art and of the corresponding imaginative forms that can give them artistic expression. Then the different formal relations between meaning and configuration get tied to differences in content that have their own ramifications for artistic shape. Instead of being external permutations visited upon the same terms, the modes of joining meaning and configuration are rather determined by the contents involved.

In this way, the artform in which meaning is too abstract to match the individuality of sensuous configuration becomes more specifically defined as the mode of artistic construal in which the self-understanding of humanity invests essential value in an ideal that lacks the individuality of independent subjectivity, directing rational agency to contemplate its own essence in alien sub-rational forms of nature or in abstract powers that transcend given existence.[2] Similarly, the artform exhibiting congruence of meaning and shape can only do so by expressing a world view that invests fundamental value in the outer manifestation of rational individuality, and accordingly, finds a perfectly adequate shape in the sensuous appearance of rational agency, shorn of physical blemishes indifferent to the expression of the soul, as well as of traces of inwardness at odds with the sphere of public worth.

What, then, is the corresponding meaning and shape with which artistic style can involve a content too concrete to be limited to any sensuous shape? Insofar as art constitutively provides a fundamental self-understanding for humanity, the relevant meaning can be determined if the world views generic to symbolic and classical art leave available but one more basic option, an option susceptible of artistic construal, and indeed, susceptible of mandating a form of expression giving art its third stylistic variety. As we have seen, symbolic art gives expression to a self-understanding of humanity that subordinates rational agency to factors devoid of the individuality of freedom, factors that can be considered naturally determined to the extent that they are given independently of the willing of the individuals to whom they apply. Classical art construes ultimate value in rational autonomy, but only as it is immediately given in sensible existence, be it in the pantheon of humanized deities or in mortal conduct pertaining to the public bonds of an ethical community, whose identity is itself defined relative to some sensuous given.[3] This leaves a third option, one overturning the last holds of natural determination by investing ultimate value in a rational agency, which, in departure from classicism, now has its autonomy freed of attachment to any particular givens of sensible existence. At last all domains of self-determination have their rights acknowledged, including the spheres of inner faith and conscience, where individuals exhibit a worth extending beyond the manifestations of their activity immediately perceivable by others. Not only does this confer equal entitlement upon all rational agents, irrespective of the sensible particulars of their appearance, such as race, gender, and birth, but it extends legitimacy to the pursuit of self-selected ends, to the degree that they can conform with those of others. Accordingly, not only do rights get extended to all competent independent rational agents, but these rights win an expanded content to include, alongside political and household entitlements, those of morality and civil society.

The ramifications for religious representation are equally familiar. Divinity will exhibit rational agency without being limited to a particular sensuous form to the extent that the divine is still honored. Hence, nature will be divested of any abiding divinity[4] and polytheism, with its attendant particularizations, will be supplanted by monotheism. Moreover, the divine will relate to individuals in respect of their autonomy, conferring absolute worth to them in their universal capacity as free agents, irrespective of their physical differences, and according them responsibility for their own integrity.[5] Consequently, the domain of the sacred can withdraw into the faith of individuals, leaving free an external secular sphere with a significance of its own. Indeed, for just this reason, the autonomy of individuals can be a focal point of concern without appeal to the divine.

Needless to say, these ethical and religious transformations comprise central agendas of modernity. This might lend support to the view that whatever artistic style is defined by shaping such a world view is not only a logical option of artistic form, but a historical stage in the development of art. However, even if modernity may be immersed in ongoing struggles to erect secular and sacred institutions conforming to the self-understanding of the third form of artistic construal, this does not guarantee that works in this style can only appear in the modern era or that art in our time can only be created in function of the prevailing world view. Artistic dissidents are no more inconceivable in any period than is the possibility of a responsive audience that bucks the tide of reigning convention. Nor does the historical emergence of such a world view preclude its eventual supplanting by any other type, together with corresponding artistic results.

Hegel, of course, identifies the above notion of rational agency with the romantic form of art and with the prosaic secular and religious aspects of modernity. As a consequence, he treats romanticism as the modern form of art per se[6] and suggests that its consummation of the logical possibilities of artistic construal also brings art to its historical culmination.

This claim is presented in concert with assertions that the conceptual ordering of symbolic, classical, and romantic artforms follows a historical necessity, and that the attainment of the romantic style brings art history to an end in that artistic creation will now be unable to break the hold of romanticism and produce in any further style. If, however, the claim of historical necessity is rescinded, romanticism can still bring the history of art to a close. So long as the romantic form is, if not posterior, at least coeval with symbolic and classical art, the advent of romanticism will represent the end of art insofar as all the modes of artistic construal will have been exercised, leaving no new modes to be explored. Art works will, of course, continue to be produced with all the originality endemic to the individuality of beauty. However, when it comes to artform, no new ground will be broken since whatever unique identity a work may have it must either match shape and configuration in classical congruence or realize the polar alternatives of symbolic or romantic discrepancy.

Yet, if the affirmation of rational autonomy in all spheres of life comprises the new self-understanding for which romanticism provides artistic form, what is the new mode of configuration that fits a world view for which no sensuous appearance can fully capture the worth of rational agency?

THE CONFIGURATION OF CONTENT IN ROMANTIC ART

Although the new self-understanding of the significance of rational agency may devalue nature and the immediate existence of individuals, external appearance remains a factor, standing as the counterpart to the subjective inner domain of conscience and belief whose centrality can no longer be ignored. With the classical unity of sensible existence and rational autonomy disrupted, both sides take on a new character, altering the scope of appearances fit for artistic construal, as well as changing their relation to the meaning they express.

Whereas the classical ideal mandated that rational agency find its complete and valid objectivity in the external manifestation of activity, romanticism offers an image of self-hood that regards immersion in sensuous appearance as a shallow debasement of the internal dimension to which the individual must now turn to give life true value.[7] Yet this rejection of an embrace of corporeality hardly necessitates a rejection of conduct and of its concomitant engagement in the world. Whereas individuals must withdraw from immediate immersion in external appearance into their own inner life to find value, they equally face the challenge of intervening in outer reality to affirm and uphold the worth of their own subjectivity, as well as that of others. Thus, just as conscience may make inner motivation the key to moral integrity, acting to realize right intentions remains imperative. If all relation to outer appearance were instead severed, the possibilities of artistic construal would be undermined.

The abiding role of corporeal existence must therefore not be neglected in determining the romantic form. Hegel might appear guilty of such omission by identifying the principle of romantic art as inner subjectivity, according to which rational agency wins its true objectivity by turning away from external existence into the depths of its own feeling, belief, and conscience.[8] Hegel characterizes the content of this spiritual elevation as an absolute inwardness, absolute insofar as it communes with itself, freed from all the particularities and external entanglements of outer life. He correlatively identifies the form of such an elevation as subjectivity aware of the primacy of its independent autonomy.[9] Such a description could suggest that romanticism is an albatross, caught with a principle whose purely inward negation of sensuous immediacy is fit for thought alone.

Hegel, however, emphasizes that the absolute subjectivity of romanticism can only retain the element of self-imposed determination that autonomy involves if it gives itself a particular actuality, breaking into external existence, even while upholding its own inwardness as the focal point of its identity.[10] Only then can the self achieve a real contrast to other selves in terms of a differentiated content it has generated in reference to its own inner life, a sin a qua non for attaining an autonomous individuation, be it as conscience or as member of a religious community of spiritual freedom.[11] It is in virtue of this dual entry into and withdrawal from sensuous manifestation that inner subjectivity can provide the principle for a form of art.

Yet what are the ways in which such inner subjectivity can give itself an outer configuration susceptible of artistic construal? Whether in regard to religious or ethical themes, the problem is the same: somehow the corporeal appearance of rational agency must reveal the indispensability of an inwardness that cannot be adequately exhibited in any particular sensible existence. As Hegel suggests, the only way sensible appearance can play such a role is by presenting an activity in which rational agency supersedes the hold of external facticity upon itself and wins an autonomous existence.[12]

Given how the content of artistic beauty in general is determined, romantic art has three basic fields for configuring inner subjectivity: the domain of religious representation and the two aesthetically appropriable realms of ethical conduct, those of a world condition of revolutionary challenge and of a world condition of settled ethical institutions. Hegel himself treats these options as the three phases of romantic art,[13] implying that they comprise a sequence both conceptual and historical. On this basis, Hegel offers a progression of stages beginning with romantic art addressing religious themes, followed next by romanticism depicting adventures of chivalry and courtly love, and concluding with a romantic art expressing what he calls the formal independence of character.[14] Such an ordering may well fit the history of Western art from medieval times through the Renaissance and into modernity, but any conceptual or historical necessity must rest on more than an empirical correspondence.

What is conceptually dictated is the tackling of the three fields of content germane to art in general. How they assume a romantic form will determine whether they represent coeval options or bona fide stages in the order of theory and/or history.

The Romantic Construal of Religious Representation

As we have seen, for religion to be susceptible of romantic construal, religious representation of the divine must shed the features that suited the world views endemic to symbolic and classical art. On the one hand, the divine must lose the abstract universality that either left it a sublime power transcending every sensuous manifestation, permitted natural forms devoid of rational agency to be invested with divinity, or reduced the configuration of rational agency to a personification of an alien god. If the independence of subjective autonomy is to be affirmed, the religious focal point for humanity can no longer lie in natural formations and cosmological processes.[15] The divine must now be sought not in nature, in which gods are no longer to be found, but in spirit, a spirit endowed with the individuality of rational agency.

Yet, because the truth of rational agency is no longer identifiable with its immediate sensuous embodiment, the classical ideal of divinity cannot be the solution for liberating the divine from nature. Although making the given appearance of rational agents the shape of divinity brings individuality and autonomy to center stage, these remain burdened by sensuous limits that particularize the divine into a pantheon of deities, whose plurality undercuts their own infinitude.

If the inner life of rational agency is to be at the center stage of religious representation, polytheism must be superseded, without, however, reducing divinity to a sublime abstraction lacking the individuality of independent subjectivity. The representation of the divine must somehow exhibit how rational agency affirms its own centrality by giving itself determinate character, while overcoming the hold of external existence. This is the challenge facing the romantic construal of religious themes.

The trinitarian drama of Christianity presents an apt, if not unique paradigm of how religious representation can convey such a movement, where the divine invests itself in a real finite individual, who, though not personifying an alien power, can retain divine status only by having his corporeal existence annulled.[16] Whereas in the classical ideal, the unity of sensible existence and rational agency rendered death something of purely negative import, death here acquires the positive significance of negating the immersion in corporeality from which spirit must arise to affirm its triumph over nature and religiously display the independent value of inner subjectivity.[17] Accordingly, a religious narrative of this type will provide a portrayal of the divine well suited for romantic construal.

As for the relation between the finite individual and the divine, it can take a properly romantic form when it is withdrawn from the externality of a perceivable interaction with a sensibly manifest deity and instead placed in the heart of the individual. There it can take a perceivable, yet purely inner form as a felt love of the divine, which can then be configurable for art through the expression pervading a figure engaged in such inward worship.[18]

In incorporating all these basic elements, as features culled from the phenomena of Christianity, Hegel's treatment is on the mark with one major caveat. Because Hegel tends to discuss the different art forms in terms of the historical phenomena exemplifying them, he illicitly implies that the conceptual development reflects an historical necessity, and that the historical examples he cites are the unique realizations of the forms they exemplify. It would be more prudent to admit that the romantic construal of the divine requires the sort of religious narrative found in Christianity, which, however, might just as well be historically realized in other faiths from yet unknown pasts and futures on earth or other planetary abodes of intelligent life.

The Romantic Construal of Conduct

On the other hand, how must the content of secular conduct be molded to fit the self-understanding expressed by romantic art? To affirm the principle of inner subjectivity, rational agents must engage in activity whose significance rests no longer simply upon its external ramifications, but essentially upon its relation to the autonomous inner aims and motives of individuals. Conversely, with nature disenchanted and naturally defined ethical community deprived of any exclusive hold upon normative conduct, the configuration of sensible existence is no longer of essential significance for rational agency. Because rational agents now find true value in the independent resolve of their own inner subjectivity, rather than in immersion in the outer appearances of conduct, the shape of the world in which they act, and the physical appearance of their own selves, are now bereft of any idealization that infuses their every feature with spirituality. Since inner subjectivity is not essentially tied to any particular sensible image of rational agency, the whole field of appearance is now left prey to contingency.[19] As a consequence, the content of conduct fit for romantic construal exhibits three basic features setting it apart from how agents and their actions get shaped for symbolic or classical art.

First, because rational agency here affirms its autonomy in overriding the hold of outer existence, the situations in which inner subjectivity manifests itself as the focal point of value can take on the most varied character. No physical environment and no dimension of the lives of individuals is either off limits or a privileged abode to the romantic artistic imagination. Since each and every set of circumstances can be a backdrop for the strivings for inner integrity, the most mundane reality can be employed for romantic transfiguration. Whereas classical art linked aesthetic worth to an ideal of beauty ridding the appearance of humanity of its contingent blemishes, romantic art extends beauty to the ugly and ordinary, in which inner subjectivity is just as much at home.[20] Because the integrity of inner subjectivity does not hang upon the immediate appearance of existence, the configuration of the world is a matter of indifference until rational agency has put its heart into some outer affair, whose external visage even then cannot provide what is essential. Accordingly, action is no longer necessitated by any specific conflict or situation. It rather proceeds from the independent resolve of individuals, who set out on adventures simply in function of their conscience, passions, and beliefs.[21] Consequently, romanticism's affirmation of the inner freedom of the individual leaves the world free to appear as its own given self.[22] In this respect, the content for romantic art is not generated by artists in the way in which creators in the symbolic and classical mold could conjure up themes nowhere encountered in experience. With the whole world the romantic artist's oyster, content can be completely prosaic in origin.[23]

Second, since autonomy is no longer subordinated to alien powers or to the realization of the externally given ends common to members of a naturally determined ethical community, agents can now reveal the gleam of their inward integrity in pursuit of the most varied self-selected particular aims. Protagonists can no longer be authors of laws and institutions, whose outer enactment is what gives their deeds significance.

Right and wrong does not reside in the external object of action, but rather in inner motivation and personal judgment.[24]

Third, since the freedom of agents is no longer limited to what their outer appearance can directly express, they now pursue their independent interests without fear of showing themselves replete with blemishes irrelevant to their inner autonomy.

These three features of the romantic construal of conduct get further qualified in terms of the two basic types of world condition that art transfigures: a "heroic" age, where the institutions of justice have yet to be instituted, and a settled world of ethical institutions, where freedom has won its self-sustaining order. Both world conditions are subject to romantic construal, even if romantic art is the preeminent modern artform, and even if modernity might be considered the age where the principles of property rights, moral autonomy, the free family, civil society, and democratic government gain universal recognition and dominant reality with the global spread of nuclear families, regulated markets, and constitutional self-government through revolution, imperialism, and anticolonialism. On the one hand, modernity may have made the institutionalization of self-determination the order of the day, but it has still been a time of struggle between competing forces where the freedoms of persons, moral subjects, family members, civilians, and citizens remain subject to restrictions linked to factors such as gender, sexual orientation, caste, race, ethnicity, religion, class, and economic inequality. Hence, even if romantic art were the exclusive prize of modernity, the modern age can still offer panoramas fitting each type of world condition.[25] On the other hand, since inner subjectivity does not depend upon outer existence for all its content, it can conceivably affirm itself either in heroic conditions of revolutionary challenge or in the pedestrian setting of a constitutional state observing all the modes of freedom.

Romantic Options in a World of Revolutionary Challenge

A world condition of revolutionary challenge presents the romantic form with a variety of ways to shape conduct. A fitting one is the scheme of chivalry, which Hegel explores at length under the rubric of the second stage in the development of romantic art. Chivalry, as a mode of conduct, fits the romantic mold to the degree that it presents knight errants pursuing self-imposed aims of personal honor, faith, fidelity, and courage, where the course of events follows the contingencies of adventure, rather than the fateful conflicts of ethical communities, torn asunder by conflicting pathos rooted in different institutions. In such sagas, what counts are not the achievement of deeds reaffirming ends existing in bonds of actual communities, but rather the singular strivings of individual protagonists, running after a glory that attaches to the affirmation of their own heart and passion.[26] It matters not whether the scene be medieval Europe, the wild west, the high seas, savage jungles, arctic wastes, or extraterrestrial outposts. In each case, chivalry can proceed provided the adventure turns upon the testing of individual fortitude in self-imposed challenges.[27] Since no objectively existing good dictates what actions to undertake, personal honor can be put on the line with regard to any occasion the protagonist judges worth the trouble. What counts as a collision engendering action is not the objective reality of a perceived injury, but rather the internal feeling of being wronged, which can be elicited by any circumstance, especially when honor and love depend upon the recognition of others.[28] Hence, the most trivial of incidents can figure as an injury to love, fidelity, or honor provoking the greatest tests of personal courage.[29] Since chivalry, thereby, proceeds from contingent situations of no inherent importance to achieve ends of a purely particular and subjective character, it tends to subvert its own high pretensions and set the stage for a comic treatment of its self-deceiving nobility.[30]

Chivalric possibilities are also possible in dramas of revolutionary upheaval, where individuals participate in founding institutions of freedom, or in dramas of reform, where protagonists struggle against particular shortcomings in existing institutions where oppression maintains a partial reign. Since chivalry can invest personal honor in punishing any perceived injury, the righting of public wrongs can readily be made a personal crusade. However, using public struggles as an occasion for testing personal honor runs the risk of trivializing the commitment to justice and thereby unveiling the formal vacuity of chivalry's absorption in being true to one's heart. Moreover, the success of revolution brings to an end the significance of chivalry to the degree that the founding of the institutions of freedom upon the ruins of overthrown tradition upholds the value of inner subjectivity through a self-sustaining objective structure no longer depending upon any singular exertion for its maintenance. By the same token, the success of reform, be it to remedy public corruption, economic inequalities, or discriminations based on gender, sexual orientation, or ethnicity diminishes the significance of the expression of inner subjectivity in some individual conduct. The righting of wrong either remains limited to single instances or else it introduces the institutional change that allows the upholding of right to be rescued from the contingent mercies of private initiative. In the first case, success translates into a purely local victory of limited and transient importance, whereas in the latter, the very scope of success removes the need for the kind of subjective engagement on which it is based.

What, then, can the romantic imagination do against a backdrop of post-revolutionary institutions, where an established political democracy, civil society, and free family institutions provide an existing order in which personal autonomy is ratified? Where, in such a world condition, can the affirmation of inner subjectivity in ***individual*** conduct any longer retain fundamental significance? Unless such individual action can still be of universal importance, the expression of inner subjectivity will be stripped of concrete universality and will have ceased to be a possible theme for artistic construal.

Romantic Options in a Post-Revolutionary World

One option for romanticism is to focus upon the periphery of the settled institutions of freedom in search of a persisting frontier where the unique appearance of individual actions still exhibits an essential value. This frontier can exist in a spatial or a temporal detachment from the prosaic reality of a constitutional state upholding all the rights and duties of individuals.

Spatially distinct frontiers can be imaginatively reached through voyages beyond the boundaries of prosaic "civilization" to either unsettled territories or to communities that lack institutions of freedom. In the former case, individuals confront one another in a situation where they stand beyond the effective reach of public institutions, despite their initial membership in self-governing states with civil societies, free families, and full recognition of moral responsibility and property rights. Whether the locale be the high seas, isolated terrestrial landscapes, or uninhabited outposts in outer space, it provides a backdrop for individuals to interact in a fortuitous "state of nature" where nothing need count more than their affirmations of conscience and belief as characters whose escape from normalcy reintroduces an opportunity for a transient chivalry.

Temporal distancing provides two alternate possibilities. On the one hand, the scene of action may be set in the period when individuals make their entry into the institutions of freedom, passing through the time of youth and apprenticeship. In that interim, individuals stand suspended between the first flexing of inner independence and the acceptance of household, social and political responsibilities. Romantic art can still find a place for inner subjectivity in this gap between the unsituated, indeterminate possibilities of youth and the "iron cage" of institutional immersion and adjustment endemic to any real engagement with the world. However, if the affirmation of personal passions, conscience, and belief may be singularly significant at that point in life, once youth is traversed and individuals occupy their roles in standing institutions of freedom, their expression of inner subjectivity in their individual deeds takes second stage to the impersonal workings of civil society and constitutional democracy.[31] The years of apprenticeship are over and the quest to make the world over in accord with youthful ideals has given way either to stubborn self-destructive refusal to adapt to the demands of mundane reality or to an accommodation allowing entry into the pedestrian roles of actual relationships.[32]

On the other hand, artistic imagination can take its protagonists on a voyage in time, withdrawing them from their place in a modern world to different ages of the past or future in which the conditions of chivalrous adventure reappear. Needless to say, what distinguishes this manoeuvre from tales of chivalry is the retention of the starting point, which casts its shadow on all that follows. Whatever adventures ensue take place in light of an abandoned world whose objective machinery of law and order belittles the significance of any single subjective striving.

This contrast becomes all the more poignant in the reverse situation, where, instead of transporting characters to spatial or temporal frontiers, romantic imagination presents the quixotic plight of anachronistic figures who affirm their inner subjectivity as if the world could still allow of chivalry.[33] In this case, the object of romantic art becomes the dilemma of attempting to uphold the centrality of a self-imposed honor in an era in which the rights of conscience and individual interest are already actualized by, on the one hand, a civil society allowing individuals to satisfy their self-selected needs in reciprocity with one another, and, on the other, by a state ruling its citizens through laws they have democratically imposed upon themselves, with due respect for freedom of belief and the importance of motive in assigning criminal guilt.[34]

Yet if spatial and temporal distancings are not relied upon to create new frontiers, what opportunities remain for romantic construal in face of functioning institutions of freedom? Indeed, the pursuit of personal honor, love, and fidelity can still be a focus for conduct, both in fulfilling one's duties as a property owner, a moral subject, a family member, an economic agent, a legal person, and a citizen, as well as in living as an outlaw. Yet, in either case, these pursuits have a diminished significance. At most, they involve purely particular aims and passions, in contrast to the universal reach of civil and political institutions, whose self-sustained constitutional operation no longer rests on any single agent or deed. Even if characters persist in holding fast to youthful strivings of world reform, the outcome will be the same. In face of the workings of police, courts, welfare administrations, and government making secure the freedoms of all, the recalcitrant apprentice will either remain a quixotic figure, whose modern knight-errantry comes too late, or a mundane activist who embraces the modalities of civil and political reform in which impersonal organizations and institutions again take center stage.[35] The portrayal of such conduct may provide entertainment or psychological edification, but hardly comprises a fit vehicle for expressing the new self-understanding of romanticism.

The Formal Independence of Romantic Character

A configuration of conduct in a post-revolutionary setting more suitable for romanticism would be one in which rational agency champions the particular content of its inner subjectivity, irrespective of its situation within a world of existing institutions of freedom. Inner subjectivity would then affirm itself in such a way that it is free of bondage to any particular external existence and thereby at liberty to utilize any embodiment with equal indifference. Each and every shape will do, so long as inwardness therein maintains its independence from exclusive confinement to any of its vestments. Inner subjectivity then manifests an autonomy detached from any existing mooring, yet restricted to a formal independence to the extent that no shape it gives itself is adequate to its freedom. Rational agency is here caught up in the private world of its own feelings and motivations.[36] Character accordingly comprises a personality defined purely subjectively through its own arbitrary amalgam of particular emotions and aims. These, as subjective, are independent of any externally given content of essential substance, such as would inform the pathos[37] of an exemplary protagonist.[38] Individuals of such character, therefore, have two basic options for affirming their governing inwardness: either they seek to realize their capricious subjective aims with the whole force of their personality or they turn inward to preoccupy themselves with the inner depths of their conscience, emotions, and beliefs.[39] No other basic alternatives are available, for if rational agency refuses to affirm the centrality of its particular inwardness in the world without, it can only turn within.[40]

In the former case, which Hegel duly analyses under the rubric of the formal firmness of character,[41] individuals act upon the world on the basis of their own contingent particularity, which they treat as independently being of highest value. However, precisely because this prized particular element of each personality is not inherently linked to any existing institutions, divinity or other external factor of universal significance, action in its pursuit is bound to encounter obstacles whose overcoming can only be a matter of accident. Hence, the portrayal of this one-sided, subjective resoluteness will entail a self-engendered adventure replete with conflicts. Its denouement does not follow the inevitable tragic trajectory of opposing pathos, but rather the contingent fate of the individual's own self-selected aims and motivations at the hands of the accidents impinging upon their attempted realization.[42] If any development can be spoken of, it pertains not to a course of events precipitated by the universal concerns of clashing ethical institutions, but rather to the transformations of the individual personality whose inner life provides the nexus of happenings.[43] Any hope of an abiding reconciliation between the world and individual's strivings to assert inner subjectivity is vain since the content of personal aims and motives is just as capricious as the fickle contingencies with which the agent must cope. Because the individual finds the fulcrum of meaning in an inner life unconnected to outer existence, the independent character of the agent has no bearing upon the events that befall him or her. They remain a blind fate with which the individual simply collides in steadfast pursuit of unyieldingly subjective ends.[44]

If, alternately, the individual be configured as one who withdraws into inner life without seeking its outward expression, the occupation of inwardness with itself can only warrant primacy if it possesses a matchless profundity.[45] In this respect, the individual must exhibit character of, to use Hegel's apt expression, an inner but undeveloped totality.[46] Yet because such individuals remain situated within the world, a world to which their inner preoccupation provides no harmonious bridge, they are liable to fall prey to colliding external contingencies with which they must make due.[47] Thus, for all its lack of outward commitment, this form of character has a twofold outer manifestation susceptible of artistic construal: first, the expression of its self-engrossed inwardness and second, the collisions it experiences in its relation to an indifferent world.

Focused inward or outward, the autonomy of such individuals remains a negative freedom, devoid of any positive external filling of inherent worth. Such, after all, is the fate of agents when they assert themselves in independence from all structures of interaction.[48] For so long as individuals choose irrespectively of the willing of others, their actions proceed in reference to the self or things, neither of which can individuate agents through a content issuing from willing. Only when individuals act in reference to what others have chosen, exercising an artificial agency whose identity is as much a product of willing as the ends it gives itself, does conduct obtain an individuation that is determined through freedom. As the romantic self-understanding can well comprehend, such reference to the willing of others can be constitutive of an "artificial" agency of moral autonomy, where individuals interact in terms of their choice of the right inner motivations. It establishes its own domain of moral responsibility, which can operate both in a world of revolutionary challenge and in the interstices of the institutions of freedom under conditions of constitutional democracy.[49]

The challenge facing romantic construal is not so much a matter of upholding the validity of this mode of freedom, but rather the question of just how significant any *individual* engagement in moral self-determination can be against a backdrop of settled institutions of freedom. Since those institutions sustain themselves through lawful self-government, individual exemplary conduct stands relegated to an example of rectitude, rather than providing the rule for life. Although constitutional institutions of freedom cannot sustain themselves unless a certain level of rectitude predominates among the citizenry, the transgressions or obedience of one individual are no longer of essential importance.

This diminished significance of individual conduct for the fabric of the ethical world is reflected in how outer appearance is here set free in an independence possessing the same formality as that of the contents of inwardness. Although the configuration of art can take any shape whatsoever and still stand as an expression of inner subjectivity, this latitude is just as much a mark of indifference, exhibiting the leveling of all configurations into dispensable vehicles of aesthetic imagination. The course of action in which inwardness reveals itself thereby becomes a contingent adventure whose circumstances and complications are as devoid of inherent significance as they are unrelated to the aims pursued in their context.[50] Since rational agency here has its agenda within itself, determined apart from the world without, what circumstances confront it are just as contingent as those in which it seeks to realize its aims.[51] In function of this relativity of both subjective ends and external environment, whatever adventures ensue comprise accidental ramifications determined independently of the protagonists' inner aims.[52] The freedom of configuration is thereby formal, lacking essential positive filling to the same degree as the inwardness it expresses. Consequently, the resulting trials and tribulations of inner subjectivity are ready made for a comic treatment, setting in relief the contingency of inner and outer and the discrepancy between the absolute claims of inwardness and the capricious character of its content.[53]

Hegel characterizes this dual determination of meaning and shape as the formal independence of individual particularities, introducing it as the third stage in the development of romantic art.[54] The differentiation of possible arenas of content for the artistic transfiguration of conduct already makes intelligible how this third form brings the determination of romanticism to completion by exhausting the remaining options for artistically construing the affirmation of inwardness. Granted that the romantic construal of religious representation and conduct in a world condition of revolutionary challenge have already been determined, the only remaining option consists in configuring conduct in a post-revolutionary world of settled institutions of freedom. In that arena, conduct can affirm inwardness either by acting upon the world with subjective resoluteness or retreating into a preoccupation with conscience, feeling, and belief.[55]

Realism, Irony, and Non-Objectivism: The End of Romantic Art

Although these may be the remaining options for romantically construing conduct in its own right in a post-revolutionary environment, romanticism can inform artistry's own expression in the work of art with the same configuration of rational agency. The same formal independence of character can be exhibited by depicting the contingent givenness of existence as an indifferent vessel for the expression of the artist's own inwardness or, conversely, by subjecting appearances to a comic manipulation, exhibiting their superfluity for the artist's inner subjectivity. With the appearance of individual conduct within a constitutional order of freedom no longer of essential importance to the affirmation of inner subjectivity, romantic art can express this very truth by embracing the given content of existence and celebrating how it, in all its indifferent detail, reflects the secured reality of inner subjectivity, or alternately, by subjecting the strivings of individuals and every aspect of reality to comic relief and subjective play. Hegel aptly suggests both as abiding options, describing how romanticism can turn to the mundane reality of humanity, forsake any attempt at idealization, and adopt a portrait-like immersion in immediate appearance, or, just as readily, unveil the comic superfluity of all appearances for the inner heart.[56]

The former option seems to put into practice the theory of mimesis, whose inability to grasp the individuality in beauty left it incapable of either justifying the value or conceiving the specificity of fine art. Hegel admits that romantic construal here reverts to imitation, but he strictly demarcates its depiction of given appearance from the edifying idealization of classicism and from the rote description of craft illustration and naturalism. In contrast to the classical appropriation of the given configuration of rational agency, romanticism appropriates the world of humanity, not in function of its inherent necessity, but in terms of its pedestrian contingency.[57] However, this portrait-like[58] embrace of the mundane is still distinct from the slavish homage to immediate appearance characterizing rote illustration and naturalism because romantic "imitation" makes an abiding attempt to infuse mundane particularity with the mark of inner subjectivity.

Without this dimension, the embrace of immediate appearances would be entirely prosaic, portraying an arbitrary subject-matter in a manner equally indifferent to its content. However, with the infusion of the inwardness of the artist, a contingent content acquires a significance that can fit its treatment. Namely, the content presents the affirmation of inner subjectivity over given appearances and does so in terms of an artistry that exhibits the subjective mastery of its creator.[59]

Such infusion can work in various ways. On the one hand, it can operate by injecting the most prosaic scene with a feeling reflecting the worth of inner subjectivity. This feeling may be manifest in the expression of rational figures who show themselves to possess an inner life accompanying the most mundane pursuits. In this way, the portrayal of the most pedestrian aspects of daily life can celebrate the independent value of inner subjectivity, as it infuses mundane personal affairs with worth independently of religious transcendence or external public undertakings.[60] Or, the feeling may reflect the view of the artist, who takes configurations of no inherent human significance and transfigures them with a felt intensity manifesting the centrality of the heart of their artistic creator. Alternately, the appropriation of given appearances can exhibit nothing but the subjective mastery of the artist, whose absorption in reproducing the most evanescent moment or the most detailed panorama celebrates an independent creativity that can affirm itself in each and every content. Or, to similar effect, individual works and styles of other artists can be appropriated to set in relief how they get newly transfigured in the imaginative play of the artist. The "discovery" of "found art," impressionism, photorealism, the aping of familiar commodities, and the "post-modern" quotations of past styles, to cite a few familiar artistic strategies, all exemplify at least in part this type of romantic construal.

Since in all these cases what is at the crux of display is the inner life of the artist, rather than the content of the objects depicted,[61] it is perfectly logical for romanticism to advance from exercising subjective mastery over the manner of representing prosaic things to gain control of the subject-matter as well.

A first step in affirming the rule of inner subjectivity over artistic theme involves imaginatively negating the putative independent significance of the outer world. Hegel duly characterizes this option as the free reign of irony, which debunks everything claiming external substance by rendering it a plaything of an unmasking artistic subjectivity.[62] This art of irony might appear to converge with comparative art, which reduced symbolic construal to an arbitrary external comparison of meaning and shape, or with satire, which dissolves the classical embrace of outer appearance by showing the world to be corrupt. However, to be a form of romantic construal, this mode of humor must do more than merely connect inherently unrelated meanings and configurations or merely annihilate the substantial worth of external existence.[63] It must also exhibit inner subjectivity in command of the objective content of art, as well as of any connection this content might have with the form of its artistic presentation.[64] Consequently, the romantic art of irony above all presents the subordination of external contents and their related forms to the particular personality of the artist, whose conscience, passions, and beliefs are given primacy.

Taken to its logical conclusion, this mastery over content can forego irony's dependence upon the themes of which it makes sport and employ completely non-objective images, whose only source of meaning is the subjectivity of the artistry they express, and the subjectivity of the audience to whose imaginative play the work is relinquished.[65] With this extreme of abstract-expressionist, non-objective art,[66] the content of art becomes a pure appearance, setting artistry itself at center stage, producing a new objective world out of its own inwardness.[67]

This complete mastering of objectivity by the creativity of inner subjectivity can be seen to persist in the post-modern artistic experiments that see themselves as supplanting the unity of the self with the endless dissemination of meaning in language and other cultural formations. Precisely because post-modernists here render the meaning of texts and figures indeterminate, they end up making all signification a matter of play, where the only arbiter is the subjectivity of the post-modern interpreter and reinterpreter of signs and inscriptions.[68] In the same way, surrealism and dada retreated behind the facade of conscious subjectivity only to resurrect the associative powers of the inner subjective imagination, where "decentered," "transpersonal" contents end up only accessible within the most inward experience.[69]

In all these variations,[70] the contrasting poles of inner subjectivity and outer configuration exhibit a common formal independence, reflecting the underlying connection between the romantic flight to inwardness and the embrace of, on the one hand, the most dogged realism, and, on the other hand, the most extreme abstract-expressionism.[71] In these ways, of which Hegel only provides a partial account,[72] the third form of romantic construal exhausts romanticism's last remaining field for artistic transfiguration.[73]

The Production and Reception of Romantic Art

The production of romantic art involves a freedom of artistic creation exceeding the autonomy of symbolic and classical artistry just as the romantic vision imbues rational agency with a self-determination surpassing any conferred upon humanity by the symbolic and classical world views. Art in the symbolic mold requires the artist to employ natural forms and personified figures to suggest an abstract essence of humanity fundamentally alien to the individual. Hence, the symbolic artist is doubly bound, first to express a content imposed from without, and second, to do so using forms whose determination could hardly count as a self-determination. Classical art, by contrast, gives artists the opportunity to acknowledge the worth of public action and to utilize their own form as the configuration of the essence of humanity. Yet they thereby are compelled to restrict the expression of their subjectivity within the confines of what can make itself immediately manifest in the body and external conduct. Hence, although classical artists are engaged in determining the sensuous appearance of their own reality, their creativity is still limited by the given shape of their immediate existence.

With romantic art, however, the artist is freed from all external restraints and enjoys the liberty to make the work of art nothing but the embodiment of his or her own creativity. This dual liberation comes to the forefront with the third form of romanticism, where the content and form of the work of art are stripped of all independent prescriptions and made wholly responsive to the artist's personal choice of how to express his or her own subjectivity.[74] With every topic and every mode of treatment at the free disposal of the artist's inwardness, the romantic creator is preeminently *self*-determining, giving determination in the work of art to what is nearest at heart with the greatest autonomy.[75] The artist, thereby, engages in an artform that has the unique character of perennially canceling its own specificity, subverting all given limits that might guide artistic creation. In this way, the romantic artist must confront more radically than any other the question of what are the proper boundaries of art, with respect to both the content of art and artistic form. Indeed, it might be more proper to say that, ultimately, the practice of romantic creation does nothing other than raise this issue ever anew, if always within a horizon that leaves art hostage to the liberty of subjective inwardness. For this reason, Danto is not entirely off the mark in suggesting that modern, that is, romantic art, converges with the philosophy of art.[76]

Accordingly, the reception of romantic art must grapple with the same fluidity of boundaries, the same arbitrariness of form and content that bedevils romantic creation. Whereas the audience for symbolic and classical art need not be plagued by doubt as to whether an object is a legitimate candidate for aesthetic appreciation, the audience for romantic art cannot avoid confronting the problem of judging how to identify art and the artistic construal of inwardness. The difficulties may be comparatively minor when encountering romantic arts of religious representation and chivalry, since these incorporate a settled content and configuration. When, however, the third form of romanticism is at hand, each act of reception may well involve a renewed judgment of where lie the limits of art.

Whatever the decision may be, once a product is identified as a work of romantic art, its audience must seek the expression of inner subjectivity and evaluate to what degree that expression has found an adequate shape. Owing to the arbitrariness with which the romantic artist, especially of the third type, molds the form and content of the artwork, aesthetic satisfaction may be difficult to find.

Romanticism and the End of Art

Given how symbolic, classical, and romantic art exhaust the three basic ways in which meaning and configuration can be united in artistic beauty, the third stage of romanticism equally consummates the determination of the particular forms of art. It brings to completion the mode of art in which the self-understanding of humanity, owing to its affirmation of inner subjectivity, is too concrete to have an adequate expression in any sensuous configuration.

Hegel, however, adds two key additions to the sense of this consummation. On the one hand, he claims that it comprises the historically final development of art, a development that must be preceded not only by the successive appearance of symbolic and classical artforms, but by the successive romanticisms of religious representation and chivalry. On the other hand, he claims that this third romantic mode not only comes last, but brings art to an end.[77]

This ushering in of art's end would be most easily plausible if all it signified is that the advent of this third mode brings to appearance all of the possible forms of artistic construal. In that case, although artists could continue to create, all further production of artworks could do no more than repeat modalities that have gone before. Such would be the situation provided that the appearance of romantic art is, if not necessarily preceded by, at least coeval with symbolic and classical art. Hegel, however, is not just denying that art can invent new modes. He is arguing both that romantic construal must come after symbolic and classical styles and that the end of art achieved by the formal independence of individual particularities signifies the elimination of the very stature of art as a vehicle of fundamental self-understanding.

The former claim of historical finality is dubious for the same reasons that undermine Hegel's claims concerning the necessary historical ordering of symbolic and classical art.[78] The world view affirming inwardness may well arise through a rejection of the symbolic homage to an abstract absolute devoid of individuality or of the classical celebration of the immediate external existence of rational agency. Yet even if this were the case, it does not guarantee that romanticism need arise in that way nor that it emerge after the other modes of artistic construal have run their course. All could conceivably coexist in an age of competing cultures or at any time among dissident creators.

However, admitting that romanticism can conceptually exhaust the possibilities of artistic construal without necessarily enjoying historical finality does not rule out Hegel's further claim that the third variety of romantic style brings art to cancel its own constitutive significance.

How, then, can the third mode of romantic art, whose form and content exhibits what Hegel characterizes as the formal independence of character, comprise a self-annulling of art? The reason Hegel offers is simple enough: because this mode construes the external circumstances of conduct to be just as contingent and willful as the aims and purposes of inner subjectivity,[79] the two sides of outer and inner relinquish the last trace of unity on which beauty depends. With rational agency withdrawing into itself and leaving the external world free to go its own way, what appearances get chosen to embody inner subjectivity has become as completely arbitrary as the content of inwardness, leaving meaning and configuration wholly external to one another.[80] The unity of artistic beauty, however, cannot subsist if shape and significance are rendered so capricious and indifferent to one another. Accordingly, Hegel concludes, romanticism's striving to configure the independence of subjectivity ends up revealing that art cannot succeed in conveying the full truth of rational agency. Although romantic art seeks to express a world view that duly comprehends the importance of inwardness, thereby attaining a truer self-understanding than its symbolic and classical counterparts, it has ended up showing the futility of its own enterprise. If humanity is to achieve genuine self-understanding, it must therefore turn away from art to some more adequate vehicle of comprehension.[81]

This alleged self-inflicted collapse of art parallels the denouements Hegel had assigned to the symbolic and classical forms at the point of their dissolutions. The comparative form of symbolic art had also sundered meaning and configuration, reducing their connection to the subjective comparison of the artist, which alone held them together. Descriptive and didactic poetry were then fittingly paraded as the artistically degenerate outcomes of that transformation, completing the separation of meaning and shape by rendering the configuration a rote portrayal entirely bereft of meaning or, alternately, rendering the significance a general teaching devoid of any necessary tie to the individual image of its presentation. Analogously, classicism's slide into satire set rational agency at odds with a corrupt world completely divested of any essential significance, leaving no external appearances worthy of expressing the value of individuals. Hence satire, like descriptive and didactic art, had a questionable aesthetic status. Yet, in each of their cases, Hegel would not go so far as to sound the tocsin for art.

What is so special about the third form of romanticism that brings Hegel to announce the end of art?

In one respect, this third form seems merely to renew the opposition with which romantic art has grappled from the outset: the opposition between external appearances set free of any immediate unity with rational agency and an affirmation of inwardness which, though requiring expression, is inherently incongruent with every outer manifestation.[82] Hence, it is tempting to conclude that the formal independence of individual particulars actually retains a unity of meaning and shape since the freedom with which external existence can be employed conforms to the arbitrariness of the content of inner subjectivity.

Hegel, however, signals the emergence of a new predicament. The romantic art of religious representation and chivalry retained some consonance between individual appearances and the affirmation of inwardness to the degree that artistic depiction of religious passion and self-imposed tests of personal worth involves specific contents of a certain kind. With the elimination of all limits upon which particulars serve to express inner subjectivity, the two sides have fallen completely apart. Now, the more subjectivity has its role enhanced, the more external appearances are deprived of inherent meaning. If the romantic artist here presents mundane reality in all its contingent givenness, this is not to reveal its ethical or divine substance, but only to use its appearance as an indifferent show of artistic virtuosity.[83] Consequently, the choice of theme and manner of depiction becomes a matter of personal arbitrariness, subjecting every objective content and form to playful manipulation and distortion by the artist's subjective mastery.[84] With romantic artistry divesting every theme and every manner of treatment of any inherent worth or any inherent connection with its counterpart, art's unity of meaning and configuration would seem to have been brought to complete collapse. If there is to be any reconciliation, it will have to occur outside art in some more suitably inward vehicle, such as religious belief or speculative thought.[85]

The lack of any further artistic alternative is readily supported by contrasting the outcome of romantic construal with that of symbolic and classical art. The comparative form of symbolic construal may well have reduced the unity of meaning and shape to a subjective connection on the part of the artist, but this predicament was predicated upon retention of a world view that sought the essence of humanity in an abstract universal. Once that self-understanding is abandoned, meaning and shape can still be reconciled in art through the classical alternative, which rejects no more than the symbolic dismissal of individuality. Similarly, when classical art arrives at undermining the unity of the essence of rational agency and its sensuous embodiment through satire's unmasking of a corrupt world, art still has an option available for reuniting significance and sensuous configuration without returning to either the symbolic or classical world views, whose artistic pursuit has led to this juncture. The romantic form provides this alternative by creating configurations that affirm the role of inwardness in rational autonomy. However, when romanticism arrives at the point of making explicit how inner subjectivity has no inherent bond with any particular appearance, it apparently looses the ability to conform to the unity of artistic beauty. No artistic solutions seem possible for it on two accounts. First, all the fundamental modes of artistic construal have already made their appearance. To this extent, no new options are available. Second, the romantic artist cannot coherently revert to symbolic and classical construal. The conceptions of humanity generic to those artforms remain repudiated by the romantic world view, whose affirmation of inwardness is not discredited by the dilemmas of romanticism. These dilemmas instead highlight the difficulty art encounters in undertaking to convey the full truth of rational agency, in which inwardness plays an essential role.

Yet do these difficulties signal the collapse of art, as Hegel suggests, or do they rather comprise the perennial challenge facing artists in a modern world? Hegel himself steadfastly grants artistic status to the two forms of romanticism that he identifies as the dual aspects of the dissolution of art. He will not deny the ascription of aesthetic worth to creations that infuse contingent given appearances with the mark of inwardness nor to those that subject all considerations of content and form to the free play of the artist.[86] In each case, a modicum of aesthetic unity persists insofar as the very contingency of the content matches the subjective mastery in the manipulation of form. Not only are subject-matter and treatment equally capricious, but both, thereby, express the same affirmation of a subjective autonomy that is not essentially wedded to any external reality. This may well signify that the object represented by art has lost all absolute interest in itself.[87] However, if what counts instead is the inner subjectivity of the artist as it triumphs over the sensible appearance of its expression, this could just as well comprise art's greatest success in conveying the truth of rational agency.

Nevertheless, even if the "end" of romantic art retains aesthetic value, its liberation of art from the hold of any given form and content still offers only a truncated view of humanity. For if inner subjectivity can only be artistically construed in an otherworldly religious dimension, in the inherently contingent personal crusades of chivalry, or in the formal independence of character as it affirms inwardness in indifference to existing institutions of freedom, art fails to grasp the full truth of how inner subjectivity comprises only an element of rational agency, an element in need of incorporation within a self-sustaining constitutional democracy. It is that incorporation that diminishes the significance of the individual appearance of conduct and that thereby leaves the romantic style with no unique image that it cannot cast aside.

5

The Challenge of Conceiving the Individual Arts

PREREQUISITES FOR A PHILOSOPHICAL THEORY OF THE INDIVIDUAL ARTS

The proliferation of arts may be a commonplace phenomena, with old arts changing and new arts arising with every novel turn in technology. Yet, just as the diverse experiments of artists demand, rather than render superfluous, an adjudication of the boundary between art and prosaic things, the parade of old, transmuted, and newborn arts equally calls into question the identities of the arts that it continually spews forth. The existence of artworks cannot of itself provide any unequivocal guidelines for demarcating one art from another or for establishing their totality. Just as the existence of individual artworks or particular styles cannot dictate which of their given features is constitutive of, and not incidental to art in general or the forms of art, so the actual appearance of arts cannot provide any necessary principles for determining the boundaries of the individual arts nor for certifying the completeness of their possible differentiation. Simply cataloguing the putative arts that have appeared may suit an empirical survey of art history, content to leave undistinguished what is contingent and what is necessary in observed facts, but it is of no consequence for systematic aesthetics.

To avoid remaining a grab bag of generalizations about given phenomena whose representative and exhaustive character can never be empirically established, a philosophical theory of the arts must free itself of bondage to the contingencies of art history and conceive what is necessarily ingredient in each individual art and determine the differentiation of arts in its entirety. These two efforts of identification and differentiation go hand in hand, since a thorough specification of arts demands some principle certifying both the completeness of their plurality and the necessary identity of each one. Consequently, if the theory of the arts is to achieve any rational necessity, it must conceive the arts as a system of individual arts, grasping their differentiation in terms of some principle certifying at one and the same time the constitutive character of each and the exhaustive scope of their plurality.

Nevertheless, for such a differentiation of the system of arts to be of significance for aesthetics, it must meet two additional requirements. First, the identity and differentiation of individual arts must issue from features that are aesthetic in character. Otherwise, the proliferation of putative arts will reflect factors indifferent to art, leaving individual arts distinguished on contingent grounds that have no necessary bearing upon any of their aesthetic features. Then the individuation of the arts ceases to be a genuine topic of aesthetics, lacking as it does any aesthetic ramifications.

Second, once differentiated through factors of aesthetic significance, the individual arts must further exhibit identities that bring to a unique reality the features of art in general and of the particular artforms. Unless what distinguishes one art from the rest involves an individual way of manifesting artistic beauty and the modes of artistic construal, the identity of the individual arts will once more be devoid of any aesthetic significance.

If either of these requirements goes unfulfilled, aesthetics will have nothing to say about the individual arts other than to acknowledge that their differentiation is of no concern for the philosophy of art. In that event, Danto, for one, would be vindicated in suggesting that delineating the structures individuating the arts would be an exercise in pedantry,[1] as barren as cataloguing artworks by weight, electromagnetic charge, or some other aesthetically extraneous consideration.

Yet where might the aesthetic factors be found that could meaningfully differentiate the system of arts and give license to a philosophy of the individual arts? To avoid begging the question, the aesthetic features from which an art must be determined cannot be unique to any individual art. Consequently, they must reside either in the determination of art in general or in that of the artforms. If the differentiation of arts issues from factors generic to artistic beauty, then the individuation of arts will be unrelated to the distinction of artforms, permitting every artform to be represented by each art.[2] Accordingly, if each individual art can realize all of the artforms within its bounds, this will testify to how the individuation of arts is rooted in the concept of art in general. By contrast, if the differentiation of arts is tied to the distinctions of artforms, then certain arts should only be capable of embodying some, but not all the forms of art.

Turning to some element in art in general as the factor differentiating the arts is heuristically supported by how art history seems to have accommodated examples of symbolic, classical, and romantic art in every putative art, save perhaps for those arts tied to technologies that have arisen in recent times, such as photography, film, and holography. What might be the factor ingredient in art in general that could serve to individuate the arts? A likely candidate, favored by traditional divisions of the arts, is the physical medium in which the work of art wins existence.

All along the categorization of art in general and of the particular artforms has involved reference to the dimension of sensuous externality, without which the artwork cannot manifest its melding of image and thought. This was true even though artistic beauty can appear directly to sensuous intuition or indirectly to imagination through the sensible appearance of language. In either case, beauty cannot appear without taking some sensible form of existence. Yet, even if artistic beauty entails a physical presence directed at the appreciation of rational agents, the concepts of art in general and of the artforms do not further qualify the physical being of the artwork. It remains a sensible presence, suitable for artistic construal, whose particular physical qualities remain otherwise undetermined. As a consequence, the categories of art in general and of the artforms do not determine this final remaining dimension of configuration whereby the artwork is concretely actualized in sensuous material.[3] Hence, until the physical presence of art is conceived in regard to its aesthetic ramifications, systematic aesthetics cannot claim to have taken due account of the sensuous existence of art. Whether this is equivalent to conceiving the system of individual arts remains to be seen.

Individuating the Arts by Physical Media

In the abstract, the media of art could be distinguished according to the types of physical properties that things can have. These kinds of physical being would have to be already established in the philosophy of nature if dogmatic reliance upon common sense or the pragmatic assurances of empirical science are to be avoided.

The most minimal way in which artistic media can be differentiated in purely physical terms is through space and time, the two elementary factors ingredient in all further dimensions of sensible reality. As Stephen

Bungay has argued,[4] defining media in respect to space and time yields six possible varieties. To begin with, artistic media can have their identity in function of or in indifference to time. For those media that are indifferent to temporal form, two further options are possible: they can either be indifferent to space or employ spatial forms. Moreover, if such media are spatially differentiated, they can form space in either two or three dimensions. In this way, three temporally indifferent arts can be distinguished: one that is also indifferent to space, one that forms space in two dimensions, and one that forms space in three dimensions. As for those media that are formed temporally, two corollary alternatives are possible: they can either be indifferent to space or formed in regard to space. And, if they are spatially differentiated, they can form space in either two or three dimensions. Accordingly, three temporally formed artistic media are possible: one that is indifferent to space, one that forms space in two dimensions, and one that forms space in three dimensions. As Bungay suggests, literature, visual art, and plastic art could fit the three alternative schema of temporally indifferent media, respectively, whereas music, film, and dance or dramatic theater could fit the three options of temporally formed media, respectively. Literature is indifferent to the temporal and spatial ordering of its expression to the degree that it relies upon the inner recreations of verbal imagination. Similarly, visual art could be considered indifferent to time yet formed in two dimensions of space to the extent that it relies upon creating static surface images, whereas plastic art could be considered indifferent to time yet formed in three dimensions of space insofar as it produces motionless corporeal shapes. Conversely, music can qualify as a temporally formed, but spatially indifferent media to the degree that it employs temporal arrangements of sonority. For its part, film, be it chemically or electronically based, can qualify as a medium forming time and space by employing moving pictures, whereas dance and dramatic theater can count as exemplars of a three-dimensional temporally formed art, expressing itself in moving figures.

Nevertheless, it is questionable whether spatio-temporal orderings are sufficient to identify such media in regard to the additional physical properties that otherwise distinguish them. If these further features are not incidental to the aesthetic significance of each putative artistic media, then a spatio-temporal schematization will not be the proper vehicle for individuating the arts. Moreover, in that case, spatio-temporality will hardly be the only principle for dividing the arts that can be derived from the concept of art.[5]

This does not mean that a division of arts can be undertaken by simply turning to other more concrete physical differences. No matter which physical factors are employed, the differentiation of arts will go astray if it neglects the non-physical dimension of the work of art to which its external reality is tied. What must not be ignored is that the external existence of the work of art is constitutively an appearance for rational agency, without which its meaning and relation of meaning and configuration remain undefined. Consequently, the types of physical media suitable for art are limited by the modes of aesthetic apprehension of the audience. The possible modes of art's physical being must accordingly be further screened in function of the capabilities of perception, imagination, understanding, and reason of rational agents. An account of these capabilities falls outside of aesthetics proper into the philosophy of mind, demonstrating anew how aesthetics can rise above dogmatic assumptions only by belonging to a system of philosophy properly categorizing the aspects of nature, mind, and ethics that aesthetics presupposes.

Since every aesthetic appearance must offer itself to the common structures of imagination, understanding and reason, these cannot serve to differentiate the arts. Consequently, the relevant modes of apprehension appear to be identical with the different senses with which rational agents may be endowed.[6] Accordingly, the different media of art could be characterized as the types of physical being apprehended by each of the senses. Granted that rational agents may be endowed with senses of sight, hearing, touch, smell, and taste, and that objects can be found or produced with physical properties registering to each of these senses, the division of arts could be made in terms of media directed at one or more of these senses. On this basis, visual art, music, culinary art, and arts of touch and smell could all be distinguished in conjunction with the mixed arts combining their salient features.

However, as the concept of art has established, not all the senses are equally competent to provide access to beauty. "Practical" senses, such as smell and taste, which apprehend only through the disintegration of their objects, cannot provide universally communicable experiences to the degree that what they perceive is changed by each apprehension. Further, a sense requiring immediate contact with its object, such as touch, remains engrossed in the singularity of its experience, hobbling the appreciation of any organized artistic form. On these grounds, touch, taste, and smell can be disqualified as proper media of art, leaving the comparatively "theoretical" senses of sight and hearing as suitable organs of aesthetic experience.

This exclusion of the "practical" senses and their corresponding physical dimensions from the realm of artistic beauty has been commonly embraced by aesthetic theorists including Kant, Schelling, and Hegel, and corresponds to the acknowledged existing spheres of fine art, from which the virtuoso creators of culinary art and perfume have been banished. Yet, this exclusion is shortsighted in one fundamental regard afflicting any merely physical division of the arts. It ignores the primary non-natural, conventional media of art, language, and the dimensions of sense by which it can manifest itself. Even if the sensuous intuitions of touch, taste, and smell cannot provide images capable of supporting the unity of meaning and configuration generic to art, they can all conceivably function as signs of a language, conveying images to the imagination of an audience that are full of poetry. Contemporary systems of braille confirm how touch can be employed to this end, and although taste and smell may be far less convenient vehicles, they too could be similarly adapted.[7] Nevertheless, this possibility does not resurrect distinct arts of touch, taste, and smell. If the touch, taste, or smell of an object must be employed as a sign to enter art, they simply become absorbed within the common fold of an art of language. However, this art, which can be defined neither as an art of sight, sound, touch, taste, or smell, still has a medium of its own, a medium that is not merely physical, but spiritual in character. For, no matter what physical being it may have for its expression, and no matter to which sense organ it appeals, an art of language employs a conventional product of mind, or, one might better say, of intersubjectivity, whose intelligibility supervenes upon its merely natural properties.

Accordingly, the division of arts by media predicated upon the different senses ends up baptizing a system of arts consisting in the visual arts, music, the art of language (that could broadly be called "literature"), and mixed arts combining these. Further differentiations of the visual arts, and at least of mixed arts containing a visual element, can then be made on similarly physical terms, employing spatio-temporal differences. The visual arts can readily be divided into graphic arts, which restrict themselves to the two-dimensional surface of their medium, and plastic arts, which employ all three-dimensions. Each can then be further divided into static and kinetic branches, depending upon whether the visual images they produce also employ temporal change as part of their composition.

Yet, is such a division of arts by the form of media, independently of content, a proper way of laying hold of aesthetically significant differences?

Kant's Division by Analogy to Speech

Since art conveys a melding of thought and image, might a more appropriate division of arts be achieved by analogy to the linguistic means with which rational agents communicate their concepts and sensations at once? Kant offers this strategy, albeit with the caveat that it is not a rigorous theory so much as the most convenient of various schemes that can be devised.[8] Granted that individuals communicate their feelings and concepts by the three concomitant dimensions of word, gesticulation, and tone, Kant suggests that the arts be similarly divided into the arts of speech, the formative arts, and the art of the play of sensations, which allegedly contains both music and an abstract art of color.[9] According to this scheme, the arts of speech, identified as rhetoric and poetry, employ words to convey ideas in conjunction with a free play of the imagination, the formative arts employ sensible intuition rather than words to express ideas, just as gesticulation provides an image to convey its meaning, and the art of the play of sensation modulates sensations representing no discursively identifiable object just as tone utilizes its own oscillations to communicate.[10] Accordingly, Kant identifies the arts of speech as rhetoric and poetry, the formative arts as painting, sculpture, and architecture, and the art of the play of sensation as consisting in the arts of tone and color.[11]

The result conforms to the familiar division of literature, visual art, and music, with one exception: the art of the play of sensations separates from painting an abstract art of color and places it on a par with music, contrary to both the unities of sense and of space and time. Be this as it may, the rationale for so dividing the arts in analogy to the elements of speech breaks down because the fusion of concept and intuition, which Kant finds both in artistic beauty and in linguistic practice, is not achieved in articulation, gesticulation, and modulation taken individually, but only by their concomitant working. Yet if word, deportment, and tone convey concept and feeling only by functioning in consort, then it makes little sense to base an art upon each individually.

Kant's grouping together of music and abstract color art (to which a monochromatic play of shape could just as easily be added) might seem better grounded in an alternative dichotomy that he briefly entertains. It divides the arts according to whether they express thoughts or intuitions, and, in the case of the arts expressing intuitions, divides these again according to whether they deal solely with form or matter.[12] This leaves literature presumably expressing thought without intuition. By contrast, this scheme distinguishes painting from the art of color to the extent that painting is representational, conveying the form or concept of its object, whereas the latter's mere play of color offers only intuitions of sensation with which the imagination and understanding might still entertain themselves.[13] Although Kant dismisses such a division as too abstract and too discordant with received practice, it fails for precisely the same reason that undermines the division in analogy with the elements of speech.

Once again, the differentiation of arts is based upon a separation of thought and intuition, of meaning and configuration, which each and every example of artistic beauty must overcome to be worthy of the name.

Does this failure mean that the division of arts should proceed upon the aforementioned differentiation of media according to the artistically viable modes of sense perception and language, as qualified by the options of spatio-temporal ordering? Although Hegel ends up identifying individual arts that could, with limited modifications, be fit into such a system, he offers a different principle of division tied to the modes of artistic construal. In so doing, he does observe the demands of categorial immanence by relying upon aesthetic factors already developed in the determination of artforms. Moreover, his analysis of each resulting art extracts aesthetically significant ramifications from the boundaries of their individuation. Yet, is any such appeal to the particular forms of art a viable gambit for establishing the system of arts?

Hegel's Division by Appeal to the Artforms

Why should the character of the aesthetically fit senses and of their corresponding sensible media be dismissed as grounds for the division of the arts, let alone, cede their differentiating role to the artforms? Hegel admits that the differentiation of the possible modes of art reception into sight, hearing, and linguistic apprehension provides the principle for the customary division of the arts into visual art, music, and literature.[14] Yet, individuating arts according to this sensuous dimension touches upon only their most abstract aspects, Hegel warns, at risk of leaving unaccounted for the details of what is aesthetically generic to each individual art.[15] Although the proof of such shortcomings would first be found in the actual individuation of the arts, Hegel points to two general features on which he rests his rejection of any division by media irrespective of content.

First, because art constitutively brings the truth of humanity to sensuous apprehension, how this occurs in the medium of external reality must be determined in function of how that truth divides itself in respect to sensuous existence.[16] In other words, the content of artistic beauty must be brought to bear upon the system of arts. If it is not, then the conception of individual arts remains bedeviled by Danto's insight that artworks could conceivably share a common material counterpart and yet belong to different arts.[17] A page of text, for instance, could just as easily count as a work of literature as as a work of visual art if one abstracts from the meaning to which it must be referred to identify its art and the corresponding guidelines that its author must heed.[18] Only when the meaning of the work is considered in conjunction with its physical/physiological character can the indiscernibility of arts be overcome. Given the constitutive unity of meaning and configuration, this must be done to determine the ramifications of different art media not only for the range of content they can convey, but equally for the kind of artistic form they can support. Nevertheless, could this not be done within the framework of the physical/physiological division, tying each media-individuated art to the unique scope of form and content it entails? Moreover, could it not be done independently of the particular artforms, such that each art could retain an identity that would persist throughout its own realizations of symbolic, classical, and romantic modes of artistic construal?

Indeed, Hegel's own account of the individual arts largely supports this option, not just because his division by artform ends up largely conforming to the traditional division by media,[19] but more importantly, because whether he is analyzing architecture, sculpture, painting, music, or literature, he shows how each of these individual arts can take on symbolic, classical, and romantic forms and yet always maintain the same distinctive range of content and form that individuates it as an art.

Nevertheless, Hegel ties the entry of content into the division of the arts to the particular forms of art. Support of this connection might be sought in Hegel's contention that the individual arts progress through the different artforms because the individual arts are what give the artforms their determinate existence.[20] However, this contention can equally imply that the arts are not individuated in respect of the artforms precisely because each art passes through symbolic, classical, and romantic stages of its own, as the only way in which the artforms get actualized. Since the artforms then figure as particularizations common to every art, some other basis is required to distinguish the arts from one another. Consequently, if the particular artforms provide the principle for how content helps individuate the arts, the division of arts must proceed by identifying each art in regard to an artform that it exclusively embodies.

Since Hegel does acknowledge that each art undergoes its own symbolic, classical, and romantic phases, he can still individuate the arts in terms of the artforms only by maintaining that each art is specially suited to realize just one artform, even if its medium may become a comparatively recalcitrant vehicle for every other artistic style. Yet can such an affinity be established, with the ranking it entails, and even if it can in certain cases, can it provide a basis for individuating all the arts into a comprehensive system?

Let it be granted that the different ways in which the content of art stands in relation to its sensuous configuration correspond with the division of artforms into symbolic, classical, and romantic styles. How then is the system of arts to be individuated upon the basis of this threefold differentiation of artforms?

Following the order by which he had introduced the artforms, Hegel claims that architecture can be identified as the art that realizes in a specific media the type of artistic construal generic to symbolic art. Symbolic construal relates form and content such that the configuration only intimates a meaning too abstractly universal to have an adequate sensuous expression. Accordingly, Hegel, argues, symbolic art constitutively works upon the sensible material provided by nature to make it into an enclosure for a self-understanding of humanity whose inner meaning can only be alluded to by this external housing.[21] In the same way, architecture comprises an art that takes natural material and employs it in such a way that it remains an inherently non-spiritual configuration that can at best *seek* to express a humane truth to which it can not fully correspond. Architecture characteristically operates in this symbolic mode by shaping natural material in its completely non-spiritual capacity as inorganic, extended matter, subject to laws of gravity. By restricting its configuration to an ordering of material in terms of its inorganic shape and mass, architecture provides the most external sensuous housing that art can provide for truth. A more familiar way of identifying architecture would be to characterize it, as Kant[22] has done, as a plastic art distinguished from sculpture by producing non-representational[23] structures having an external use as an enclosure or setting for some human activity. Hegel, however, has here attempted to distinguish architecture's treatment of material by how it relates content to form,[24] avoiding appeal to the seemingly aesthetically extraneous consideration of the use to which the architectural work is put.

Accordingly, when Hegel identifies sculpture in distinction from architecture, he must characterize the sculptural shaping of matter through a different relation of meaning and configuration, narrowing what otherwise might be thought to be the limits of sculpture. Hegel attempts this by introducing sculpture as the art fitting the classical ideal.[25] On this basis, sculpture becomes a medium for presenting a self-understanding of humanity that is in perfect unity with rational agency's sensible appearance. As such, sculpture gets limited to presenting a bodily figure fully expressing a spiritual individuality with no hidden inwardness. In contrast to the architectural employment of inorganic material in non-representational orderings of heavy matter, sculpture here shapes material into the form of rational agency, a form idealized so that everything appearing on its surface makes manifest the substantial individuality of the agent, without, however, hinting at any residual spark of conscience or belief that might lie concealed within.[26]

Such a characterization seems to do violence to sculpture on two accounts. In the first place, it appears to arbitrarily restrict sculpture to representation of the figure of rational agency, and indeed, in light of Hegel's conflation of homo sapiens with finite rational agency, to representation of the human figure. Moreover, it restricts the sculptural representation of rational agency to a classical ideal, eradicating all incidental blemishes and embalming the figure in a serene tranquility from which all clue of an inner life is banished.

In Hegel's defense, it might be countered that the restriction of sculpture to representations of rational agency is not arbitrary. On the one hand, it might be argued, non-representational sculpture is entirely architectural in character, especially when the use of architectural structures for human activity is judged to be extraneous to their aesthetic character. On the other hand, if sculpture were to represent inorganic or non-rational organisms, not as scenery for human figures, but by themselves, sculpture, one might maintain, would lack a content capable of providing the self-understanding of humanity to which the dignity of art is tied.

Similarly, it could be argued that a classical idealization of the figure is something generic to sculpture because color differentiation is incidental to sculptural treatment of material and because the sculptural artwork is static and detached, freezing the figure it represents into one immobile pose removed from any comparably shaped situation. While banishing transience and location from the figure,[27] these features suppress all trace of an inner animation lying hidden within.

Such arguments are far from convincing. Admittedly, non-representational sculpture may not be distinguishable from architecture if one abstracts from the element of use and grants that architecture is not limited to some particular set of shapes or materials. However, independent sculptures of plants or animals cannot be disqualified as art owing to their content since symbolic and romantic construal can readily employ non-human figures to allude to truths about humanity. Moreover, even if one grants that kinetic and polychrome sculpture are mixed creations incorporating elements from other arts, immobility and monochromaticism do not prevent sculptures in a romantic vein from portraying individuals whose blemished and searching look reveals an inwardness transcending immediate appearances.

In a similar vein, the possibility of classical and romantic embodiments haunts Hegel's identification of architecture in terms of the symbolic artform. Architecture might well be limited to shaping material as an inorganic extended mass subject to the necessities of mechanical organization, leaving its medium at farthest remove from the reality of rational agency. Yet this alone does not dictate that the association of meaning with architectural shape must be restricted to symbolic construal. Hegel's own analyses of the Greek temple and the Gothic cathedral substantiate how architecture can fittingly configure classical and romantic ideals by playing upon the relations of interior and exterior spaces and their resonance with the activities they enclose.

If a differentiation of architecture and sculpture in terms of symbolic and classical artforms is therefore problematic, does Hegel's characterization of a third branch of art issuing from a romantic mold fare any better? Hegel claims that a final ensemble of arts can be identified as media that specifically configure the inwardness of rational agency.[28] These comprise painting, music, and literature,[29] which in this very order allegedly achieve a progressive interiorization of the art medium in ever increasing kinship with the romantic ideal.[30]

Painting begins the process by canceling the extension of bodily figure with which architecture and sculpture had labored and by rendering external shape a recreation of inner subjectivity, which not only is responsible for making a two-dimensional surface convey three-dimensional space, but also for apprehending the resulting illusion. Moreover, the idealization of extension by painting's employment of light and color allows this art to seize control of visible appearance, piercing the limited range of plastic art to convey the most encompassing panorama or the most nuanced detail of a fleeting moment. In this respect, painting is suited to configure the whole range of personal feeling, passion, and resolve, as set against the most varied backdrops, whose own contingent character vis-à-vis inner subjectivity can now be done justice.[31]

By contrast, music not only dispenses with corporeal extension, but forgoes the extension of surface images as well. Employing sonority, music takes that external phenomena which is indifferent to extended matter and visibility and which equally cancels its own presence the moment it is expressed by following the flow of time. In this respect, Hegel maintains, music's configuration of sound provides a medium paralleling the flow of shapeless feelings in the inner life of subjectivity. Whereas painting could capture inwardness as embroiled in actions immersed in a concretely pictured situation, music concentrates itself exclusively upon the non-discursive inner dimension of rational agency, restricting itself to the immediate expression of suitably significant feeling and of the character it reflects.[32]

Literature,[33] the art of language, carries the interiorization of artistic medium to its maximum, employing words whose meaning and configuration comes to life in the inner imagination of speaker and listener alike, rendering the external expression of language a subordinate, yet necessary element of its communication.[34] This development allegedly provides a perfect match for the romantic ideal on two correlative accounts. On the one hand, by taking language as its medium, literature adopts the inner voice of subjectivity in the full breadth of its discursive wealth. Whatever consciousness can verbalize of its personal experience is now immediately appropriable. Moreover, the sound and rhythm of words allows literature to draw upon some of the expressive possibilities by which music can convey feeling.[35] Conversely, linguistic imagination, unhampered by the physical limits of the other artistic media, can conjure up the widest range of actions and situations together with the most concrete evocations of character. In this respect, it not only allows for duly conveying the life of inner subjectivity, but also permits expressing the complete contingency of circumstances in which personal conscience and belief undergoes its trials.[36] As Hegel points out, literature, in winning this breadth of portrayal of rational agency, equally loses the immediacy of sensuous images, be they visual or auditory, with all the singular detail they contain.[37] Yet that mixed result is precisely in accord with the discrepancy of meaning and configuration in romanticism, where the self-understanding of humanity transcends any merely sensuous embodiment.

Significantly, the differentiation of these three "romantic arts" from one another does not issue from divisions within the romantic ideal, but rather from the physical/physiological and intersubjective factors by which a two-dimensional static visual art, music, and literature can be distinguished.[38] Consequently, when Hegel claims that the five arts of architecture, sculpture, painting, music, and literature comprise the conceptually necessary system of arts, from which imperfect and hybrid arts such as gardening, dancing, and opera must be distinguished,[39] the division of artforms can no longer masquerade as the ground individuating the arts.

Moreover, even if painting, music, and literature possess the interiorizing features that romanticism may find so congenial, these same features are all readily appropriable for symbolic and classical construal, as Hegel's own accounts help testify.

Painting's powers of illusion are opportune resources for the allusive transfigurations of the symbolic imagination, whether they take the form of grotesque exaggerations of natural forms, blank personifications of abstract deities, or enigmatic comparisons. Similarly, whatever be the achievements of ancient Greek painting on pottery or fresco, there is nothing in the pictorial resources of painting to prevent classically idealized figures from enjoying a concrete depiction of their situation far outstripping the capabilities of classical sculpture. It should also be recognized that, contrary to Hegel's omission of abstract art, painting can serve the romantic ideal without having to be representational, just as sculpture can serve classical or romantic styles without having to represent the human figure.

For its part, music can employ the repetitive variations of minimalism to convey a subjectivity shedding its individuality as an illusory skin just as readily as it can employ forms of harmonic and melodic development to express a substantial individuality in the classical mold.

And literature, in each and every one of its genres, can hardly fail to serve symbolic and classical forms when language offers the imagination the widest freedom over theme and treatment.

Repeatedly treating the merely physical character of each art as if it could be unequivocally tied to a specific content, Hegel seems to have forgotten the role of recognition in the unity of meaning and configuration he otherwise so strongly emphasizes. Although a certain physical modality may offer certain specific possibilities for the expression of different world views, a type of physical configuration cannot itself dictate which self-understanding it will serve. Although the configuration is related to its content, that content cannot be read off the shape's physical attributes without bringing into play the relation to the audience and the associations of meaning that come to life therein.

On all these accounts, Hegel's professed strategy of differentiating the system of arts by appeal to the artforms suffers an ignominious collapse.[40]

The Prospects for a Systematic Division of the Arts

If neither Kant's analogy to speech nor Hegel's appeal to the artforms can provide a ground for systematically individuating the arts, where is aesthetics to turn in bringing the categories of artistic beauty and the artforms to bear upon the actualization of art in its different media? Must we conclude that no single principle can differentiate the arts[41] and that only a pragmatic division is possible?

Resignation is unwarranted, for already, systematic aesthetics has provided the basic distinctions permitting the arts to be individuated. What is required is only a painstaking attempt to conceive how the features of art in general and of the particular modes of artistic construal get further qualified in respect to the possible types of existence that works of art can take. If due account is taken of the varieties of sense and the corresponding modes of physical existence, of the limitations that artistic beauty puts upon the employment of the senses in art, and of the spatio-temporal orderings that could have aesthetic ramifications, three basic individual arts arise.

First, there will be non-verbal visual art, divisible into two-dimensional and three-dimensional varieties that each have their static and kinetic divisions. It will thus include two-dimensional static visual art such as painting, two-dimensional kinetic visual art such as silent, non-verbal film or video, three-dimensional static visual art such as static sculpture and architecture (whose distinction might rest upon reference to the use of architectural structures), and three-dimensional kinetic visual art such as unaccompanied dance or silent non-verbal moving holograms.

Second, there will be music, which, to be addressed in its specificity, will be devoid of lyrics or verbal program.

Third, there will be literature in all those forms that remain unadorned by illustrations, music or other non-literary accompaniments.

A systematic treatment of these candidates will inquire into the aesthetic ramifications of their medium, first in regard to the features generic to art, and then in respect to how these candidates differentially actualize the distinct forms of artistic construal. Only once this is accomplished, will it be possible to assess the aesthetic character of arts combining features of these three primary arts, such as verbal visual art (be it static or kinetic and two- or three-dimensional), theater (as endowed with a visual staging and/or music), and the like.

Needless to say, this enterprise is no more unheralded than any other dimension of systematic aesthetics. In particular, Hegel has provided a vast analysis of the individual arts going well beyond the limits of the appeal to the artforms that otherwise obscures his achievement. To what degree Hegel's efforts pave the way for our own remains to be seen.

Notes

INTRODUCTION

1. F. W. J. Schelling, *The Philosophy of Art*, trans. by Douglas W. Stott (Minneapolis: University of Minnesota Press, 1989); G. W. F. Hegel, *Lectures on Aesthetics*, in two volumes, trans. by T. M. Knox and W. Miller (Oxford: Oxford University Press, 1975).

2. Friedrich Schlegel, *Über das Studium der griechischen Poesie* (Paderborn: F. Schoningh, 1982); Friedrich Schiller, *On Naive and Sentimental Poetry and On the Sublime: Two Essays*, trans. by Julius A. Elias (New York: F. Ungar, 1967); Friedrich Nietzsche, *The Birth of Tragedy and The Case of Wagner*, trans. by Walter Kaufmann (New York: Random House, Vintage Books, 1967).

3. Theodor W. Adorno, *Philosophy of Modern Music*, trans. by Anne G. Mitchell and Wesley V. Blomster (New York: Seabury Press, 1973); Walter Benjamin, *The Origin of German Tragic Drama*, trans. by John Osborne (London: Verso, 1985); Georg Lukács, *The Theory of the Novel*, trans. by Anna Bostock (Cambridge: MIT Press, 1971); Charles Rosen, *The Classical Style* (New York: W.W. Norton, 1972).

4. For an investigation of the defining logic and limits of the metaphysical approach in aesthetics, see Richard Dien Winfield, "The Individuality of Art and the Collapse of Metaphysical Aesthetics," *American Philosophy Quarterly*, Vol. 31, No. 1, January 1994, 39–51; and Richard Dien Winfield, *Systematic Aesthetics* (Gainesville: University Press of Florida, 1995), Chapter 1.

5. For an analysis of the indwelling logic and aporias of the transcendental approach in aesthetics, see Winfield, *Systematic Aesthetics*, Chapter 2.

6. See Immanuel Kant, *Critique of Judgment*, trans. by Werner S. Pluhar (Indianapolis: Hackett, 1987), Ak. 242–43, 93. Gadamer analogously discusses how Kant takes such "nonsignificant" beauty to be paradigmatic. See Hans-Georg Gadamer, *The Relevance of the Beautiful and Other Essays*, trans. by Nicholas Walker (New York: Cambridge University Press, 1986), 18–20, 164.

7. See Michael B. Foster, *The Political Philosophies of Plato and Hegel* (Oxford: Oxford University Press, 1968) 185–87, 201; and for further discussion, Richard Dien Winfield, "The Individuality of Art and the Collapse of Metaphysical Aesthetics" and *Systematic Aesthetics*, Chapter 1.

8. For a detailed exposition of these limitations, see Winfield, *Systematic Aesthetics*, Chapters 1 and 2.

9. For further discussion of these points, see Richard Dien Winfield, *Systematic Aesthetics*, Chapters 5 and 6, as well as Richard Dien Winfield, "Natural Beauty and The Philosophy of Art", *The Journal of Speculative Philosophy*, Vol. 9, Issue 1, February 1995, 48–62.

10. For further discussion of these points, see Richard Dien Winfield, *Systematic Aesthetics*, Chapters 7 and 8.

11. For an attempt to develop them further see Winfield, *Systematic Aesthetics*, Part II.

CHAPTER 1

1. Stephen Bungay, *Beauty and Truth: A Study of Hegel's Aesthetics*, (Oxford: Oxford University Press, 1987).

2. Bungay, *Beauty and Truth*, 64.

3. Bungay, *Beauty and Truth*, 52.

4. Bungay, *Beauty and Truth*, 59, 64.

5. Bungay, *Beauty and Truth*, 61.

6. Bungay, *Beauty and Truth*, 54–55.

7. Meyer Shapiro describes a variety of such efforts in his essay, "Style", in *Aesthetics Today*, edited by Morris Philipson and Paul J. Gudel (New York: The New American Library, 1980), 151ff.

8. G. W. F. Hegel, *Lectures On Aesthetics*, trans. by T. M. Knox and W. Miller (Oxford: Oxford University Press, 1975), II, 615–21.

9. Hegel, *Lectures On Aesthetics*, II, 615.

10. Hegel, *Lectures On Aesthetics*, II, 616–19. Gillian Rose suggests that the "pleasing style" comprises a form of the end of art, which supersedes the opposition between meaning and configuration in romantic art with an embrace of given shape. (Gillian Rose, *Hegel Contra Sociology* {New Jersey: Humanities, 1981}, 142.) Yet since the "pleasing style" aims to gratify the audience by emphasizing the charm of configuration at the expense of meaning, it seems more of a deformation than a form of artistic expression. Moreover, the "pleasing style" bears no special relation to romantic art, in which it is the configuration that finally becomes a matter of indifference with respect to the meaning.

11. Consequently, Peter Szondi is wrong to suggest that Hegel's distinction of severe, ideal, and pleasing styles recapitulates the division of artforms into symbolic, classical, and romantic modes of artistic construal. See Szondi, *Poetik und Geschichtsphilosophie I* (Frankfurt am Main: Suhrkamp, 1974), 466.

12. Bungay, *Beauty and Truth*, 57–58.

13. Meyer Shapiro points out how art historians have joined philosophers of culture in making the analogous assumptions that "every style is peculiar to a period of a culture and that, in a given culture or epoch of culture, there is only one style or a limited range of styles." See Meyer Shapiro, "Style", in *Aesthetics Today*, 138.

14. In Hegel's introductory remarks to his analysis of the system of individual arts, he describes different types of artistic style that are not distinguished in terms of world views and corresponding configurations, but in terms that allow them to apply both to each artform, as well as to each individual art. The significance of these styles in regard to the differentiation of artforms will be discussed in the next chapter.

15. See Friedrich Schiller, *On Naive and Sentimental Poetry and On the Sublime: Two Essays*, trans. by Julius A. Elias (New York: F. Ungar, 1967), 106ff; F. W. J. Schelling, *The Philosophy of Art*, trans. by Douglas W. Stott (Minneapolis: University of Minnesota Press, 1989), 91–93.

16. Admittedly, both Schiller and Schelling grant that certain modern figures, such as Shakespeare, introduce features of naive art in their works.

17. Meyer Shapiro, "Style", in *Aesthetics Today*, 149.

18. Meyer Shapiro, "Style", in *Aesthetics Today*, 146.

19. See Meyer Shapiro, "Style", in *Aesthetics Today*, 139.

20. Consequently, the linkage between form and content in the different modes of artistic construal does not render the artforms historical, rather than systematic categories, as Szondi erroneously suggests in his parallel treatment of lyric, epic, and drama. See Peter Szondi, *The Theory of the Modern Drama*, trans. by Michael Hays (Minneapolis: University of Minnesota Press, 1987), 4.

21. This claim runs counter to the increasingly fashionable notion, advanced with self-referential blindness by thinkers from Heidegger to Rorty, that post-modern philosophy undercuts its own capacity to arrive at truth and hands over the task of achieving self-understanding to art.

22. Hegel, *Lectures On Aesthetics*, I, 300.

23. Consequently, recognition of the constitutive connection between form and content in art and of its different modes, does not eliminate the possibility of a "systematic, that is, a normative, poetics," as Szondi mistakenly claims. See Szondi, *Theory of the Modern Drama*, 5. Indeed, Szondi's own treatment of the transformations of form and content in modern drama exhibits a systematic development in which the aesthetic problems of different dramatic genres become progressively more acute.

24. See Richard Dien Winfield, *Systematic Aesthetics* (Gainesville: University Press of Florida, 1995), Chapters 6 and 7.

25. Curtis L. Carter provides a rare example of an interpreter who examines the "death of art" thesis in light of how the symbolic, classical, and romantic artforms are ahistorical modes of artistic construal. See Curtis L. Carter, "A Re-Examination of the 'Death of Art' Interpretation of Hegel's Aesthetics" in *Art and Logic In Hegel's Philosophy*, edited by Warren E. Steinkraus and Kenneth I. Schmitz (New Jersey: Humanities Press, 1980), 83–100.

26. Humanity, it bears noting, here represents the community of rational agents, be they homo sapiens or members of some intelligent species that humans have yet to encounter.

27. If instead, what were at stake were deriving the social preconditions for the artforms from instances of these forms, as Gillian Rose maintains that Hegel is doing, (see Gillian Rose, *Hegel Contra Sociology* {New Jersey: Humanities Press, 1981}, 123.) the bounds of systematic immanence would be broken, giving free rein to unjustified appeals to historical givens. The dogmatism afflicting any such "transcendental" account of the artforms can only be surmounted by locating the basis of differentiation in factors inherent in artistic beauty as such.

28. In his interpretation of Hegel, Gillian Rose describes the symbolic form of art as that which arises in a society where nature is revered as divine, exhibiting a universal power in its natural givenness. Because the natural object can only denote the absolute in an incomplete way, the symbolic artform neither *presents* nor *re-presents* the absolute, but makes reference to it abstractly and indeterminately, in the ambiguous manner of symbolization. (Rose, *Hegel Contra Sociology*, 146.) As Rose indicates, Hegel does tie the symbolic form to a world view where what is of fundamental significance to humanity is still invested in natural determination devoid of proper subjectivity. Nevertheless, it must be established whether this apotheosis of nature exhausts, or is but one manifestation of, the option where the meaning of art is too abstract to conform to any sensuous configuration.

29. Hegel, *Lectures On Aesthetics*, I, 300.

30. Hegel, *Lectures On Aesthetics*, I, 303.

31. Hegel, *Lectures On Aesthetics*, I, 301.

32. Hegel, *Lectures On Aesthetics*, I, 301.

33. See Rose, *Hegel Contra Sociology*, 131.

34. Hegel, *Lectures On Aesthetics*, I, 301–302.

35. Hegel, *Lectures On Aesthetics*, I, 302. Gillian Rose maintains that romantic art thereby no longer simply *presents* its meaning in the immediate fashion of classical art, but instead reverts to a *re-presentation*, whose autonomous illusion reproduces the disunity of a prosaic world condition, conveying anew truths already independently established in religion and philosophy. (See Gillian Rose, *Hegel Contra Sociology*, 136–42.) However, it can be questioned whether the prosaic world, whose orientation allegedly belongs to romantic art, need be a dirempted domain ruled by instrumental reason and deprived of ethical community, as Rose suggests, just as it can be questioned whether the relation between meaning and configuration in romantic art is a re-presentation or rather an employment of images of a different sort.

36. Vittorio Hösle, *Hegels System—Band 2: Philosophie der Natur and des Geistes* (Hamburg: Meiner Verlag, 1988), 619–22.

37. *Ibid.*, 620–22.

Chapter 2

1. Hegel, *Lectures On Aesthetics*, I, 314.

2. Hegel, *Lectures On Aesthetics*, I, 314.

3. Hegel, *Lectures On Aesthetics*, I, 303.

4. Hegel, *Lectures On Aesthetics*, I, 303, 314.

5. Hegel, *Lectures On Aesthetics*, I, 303.

6. Hegel, *Lectures On Aesthetics*, I, 304–305.

7. Admittedly, the connection is not given apart from how the expression already functions within a system of reference.

8. Hegel, *Lectures On Aesthetics*, I, 305.

9. Hegel, *Lectures On Aesthetics*, I, 305–306.

10. Hegel, *Lectures On Aesthetics*, I, 306.

11. Hegel, *Lectures On Aesthetics*, I, 306.

12. Hegel, *Lectures On Aesthetics*, I, 306.

13. Hegel, *Lectures On Aesthetics*, I,307.

14. Hegel, *Lectures On Aesthetics*, I, 307.

15. In this way, Hegel maintains, the understanding is prone to destroy the form of art by tending to interpret each artistic creation as a symbol or allegory, where image and meaning are set apart. See Hegel, *Lectures On Aesthetics, I*, 312.

16. Hegel, *Lectures On Aesthetics*, I, 314.

17. Hegel, *Lectures On Aesthetics*, I, 309.

18. Hegel, *Lectures On Aesthetics*, I, 313.

19. Hegel, *Lectures On Aesthetics*, I, 313.

20. Hegel, *Lectures On Aesthetics*, I, 308.

21. Hegel, *Lectures On Aesthetics*, I, 437.

22. Hegel, *Lectures On Aesthetics*, I, 439.

23. Hegel, *Lectures On Aesthetics*, I, 478.

24. Hegel, *Lectures On Aesthetics*, I, 315–16.

25. Hegel, *Lectures On Aesthetics*, I, 315–16.

26. As Peter Szondi points out, Hegel's argument here underscores how art presupposes a duality of meaning and shape, without which the appreciation of putative works of art gives way to direct worship of nature and fetish objects. See Peter Szondi, *Hegels Lehre von der Dichtung* in *Poetik und Geschichtsphilosophie I*, 372.

27. Hegel, *Lectures On Aesthetics*, I, 316.

28. Hegel, *Lectures On Aesthetics*, I, 316.

29. Hegel, *Lectures On Aesthetics*, I, 314.

30. Hegel, *Lectures On Aesthetics*, I, 317.

31. Hegel, *Lectures On Aesthetics*, I, 317.

32. Hegel, *Lectures On Aesthetics*, I, 318.

33. Hegel, *Lectures On Aesthetics*, I, 318.

34. Hegel, *Lectures On Aesthetics*, I, 318. For an extended account of why the reality of freedom can alone possess fundamental validity, see Richard Dien Winfield, *Reason and Justice* (Albany: State University of New York Press, 1988), Part III.

35. Hegel, *Lectures On Aesthetics*, I, 318–19.

36. Hegel, *Lectures On Aesthetics*, I, 319.

37. Hegel, *Lectures On Aesthetics*, I, 333, 340.

38. Hegel, *Lectures On Aesthetics*, I, 318.

39. Hegel, *Lectures On Aesthetics*, I, 333.

40. Hegel, *Lectures On Aesthetics*, I, 319, 333.

41. Hegel, *Lectures On Aesthetics*, I, 319.

42. Hegel argues that unconscious symbolism, in its exemplification in ancient Indian art, so completely identifies the sensuous thing with universal meaning that it violates the fundamental edict of symbolic construal, that the particular thing providing the configuration not actually be the absolute meaning, but only indicate it to us. (Hegel, *Lectures On Aesthetics*, I, 337.) Yet even if the ape, the cow, and the individual Brahman are treated and represented as the Divine, this does not signify that their employment as images in the mode of unconscious symbolic art eliminates their status as recognizable appearances in a work of art, which, as such, sets them in the framework of aesthetic reception. In that framework, the image retains its role as indicator of a meaning whose expression may depend upon it, but not be identical to it.

43. Hegel, *Lectures On Aesthetics*, I, 318–19, 429.

44. Hegel, *Lectures On Aesthetics*, I, 318.

45. Admittedly, Hegel already introduces such distortions in describing how, as exemplified in ancient Indian art, unconscious symbolism operates once it recognizes how it links abstract universal meanings to completely incompatible sensuous individuals. See Hegel, *Lectures On Aesthetics*, I, 334.

46. Hegel, *Lectures On Aesthetics*, I, 319.

47. In Hegel's analysis of ancient Indian art within his account of unconscious symbolism, he already introduces a mode of representation that distorts and exaggerates given appearances to express an absolute meaning with an element of sublimity. However, Hegel maintains that such a mode of representation is not strictly symbolical since, on the one hand, symbolism proper allows the image it employs to remain as it is given, and, on the other hand, symbolism does not treat the immediate existence of the shape to be the meaning, but rather suggests the meaning through reference to certain properties of the shape. (Hegel, *Lectures On Aesthetics*, I, 339.) Similarly, he claims that such art falls short of genuine sublimity, since sublimity requires that the absolute entirely withdraw from the appearance by which it is conveyed, whereas Indian art remains enamored of its expansive configurations, identifying the absolute with them. (*Ibid.*, I, 339–40.) However, it is questionable whether the symbolism in symbolic art must leave its shapes as they are given in experience, or whether a mode of rep-

resentation that distorts its shapes beyond their natural configuration need retain the positive relation to them that falls short of sublime art.

48. Hegel, *Lectures On Aesthetics*, I, 320–21.

49. Hegel, *Lectures On Aesthetics*, I, 319.

50. Peter Szondi maintains that sublime art's coincident positing and sublating of sensuous reality is only possible in speech, permitting poetry, but not painting or sculpture, to bring the art of the sublime to appearance. (Peter Szondi, *Poetik und Geschichtsphilosophie I*, 382.) If this were the case, sublime art would not be a stage of symbolic art per se, but rather a feature of how symbolic art gets realized in the arts of speech. The preceding account should indicate, however, that the art of the sublime can be differentiated from other modes of symbolic construal without introducing features of an individual art, such as poetry. How individual arts other than poetry realize sublime construal within their own spheres can only be systematically addressed in the theory of artistic genres, where the individual arts are determined.

51. Hegel, *Lectures On Aesthetics*, I, 320–21.

52. Hegel, *Lectures On Aesthetics*, I, 319.

53. In this regard, it is worth noting that Hegel locates the art of sublime pantheism in three historically distinct cultures, noting its appearance in ancient India, in mystical Islamic art, and in phenomena of Christian mysticism. (Hegel, *Lectures On Aesthetics*, I, 321.) Moreover, he identifies the three major stages of symbolic art, unconscious symbolism, sublime art, and comparative art, with, respectively, (*Ibid.*, I, 320.) the ancient Parsi religion, ancient India, and ancient Egypt, which hardly allows the conceptual succession of these varieties of symbolic art to correspond with a historical succession. Hegel himself accounts for this haphazard historical recurrence of different artforms as being due to how the individual manners of configuration are as mixed as the artforms themselves. (*Ibid.*, I, 320.) A more compelling reason would be that the differentiation of artforms is simply conceptual and does not dictate any necessary historical ordering to their appearance.

54. Hegel, *Lectures On Aesthetics*, I, 318–19.

55. Hegel, *Lectures On Aesthetics*, I, 321.

56. Hegel, *Lectures On Aesthetics*, I, 318.

57. Hegel, *Lectures On Aesthetics*, I, 421, 437.

58. Hegel, *Lectures On Aesthetics*, I, 319–20.

59. Hegel, *Lectures On Aesthetics*, I, 422.

60. Hegel, *Lectures On Aesthetics*, I, 321.

61. Peter Szondi raises doubts about the suitability of these candidates

for the final stage of symbolic art. See Peter Szondi, *Poetik und Geschichtsphilosophie I*, 391 ff.

62. Hegel, *Lectures On Aesthetics*, I, 321, 512.

63. Hence Hegel can claim that even here in comparative art, meaning and shape still have a bearing upon one another, as the essence of art mandates. See Hegel, *Lectures On Aesthetics*, I, 422. He equally maintains that this bearing is no longer symbolic in character, since it supposedly attempts to cancel the incompatibility of meaning and shape that the other forms of symbolic art could not surmount. (*Ibid.*, 422). However, he admits that since the separation of significance and configuration is presupposed by comparative construal, its attempt at uniting them remains an imperative. (*Ibid.*, 422.) Thus, instead of advancing beyond the framework of symbolic construal, where the union of meaning and shape never eliminates their incongruence, comparative art remains within the fold. Although Hegel claims that the purpose of his analysis of these kinds of comparative art is to clarify the transition from the symbolic to the classical art form, (*Ibid.*, 422.), it remains unclear how they bring us any closer to the classical achievement of congruence in meaning and shape.

64. Hegel, *Lectures On Aesthetics*, I, 322.

65. Hegel, *Lectures On Aesthetics*, I, 322.

66. Significantly, Hegel acknowledges the place of didactic poetry in the art of ancient Rome, which he otherwise characterizes as providing a bridge between the classical form of ancient Greek art and the romantic form of Christian art. See Hegel, *Lectures On Aesthetics*, I, 515.

67. Hegel, *Lectures On Aesthetics*, I, 423.

68. Hegel, *Lectures On Aesthetics*, I, 424.

69. Hegel, *Lectures On Aesthetics*, I, 425.

Chapter 3

1. Of course, how the content of art can be too concretely universal to be adequately expressed in an image remains to be examined as a primary topic in the determination of the romantic form of art.

2. Hegel, *Lectures On Aesthetics*, I, 428.

3. Hegel, *Lectures On Aesthetics*, I, 429–31.

4. Hegel, *Lectures On Aesthetics*, I, 440.

5. Needless to say, these reflections anticipate features of classical and romantic art that await their systematic treatment.

6. Hegel, *Lectures On Aesthetics*, I, 441.

7. Hegel, *Lectures On Aesthetics*, I, 441–42.

8. Hegel, *Lectures On Aesthetics*, I, 442.

9. Hegel, *Lectures On Aesthetics*, I, 477.

10. Hegel, *Lectures On Aesthetics*, I, 477.

11. Hegel, *Lectures On Aesthetics*, I, 433.

12. As Danto would maintain, it still may be possible for the same configuration that suits classicism to figure as a prosaic thing or as an element incorporated within a work of romantic art expressly referring to classical forms for other artistic purposes. Yet this still does not prevent specific shapes from unambiguously fitting certain meanings, provided the context of artistic presentation sets them together. That this context is a precondition of their congruity in no way undermines the internal character of their fit. The relation of meaning and configuration may function only within a framework of representation, but that framework does not unilaterally dictate what is possible within its field.

13. For this reason, Hegel aptly describes the fundamental characteristic of classical art as consisting in a free independence, where the content and its configuration are each a totality possessing the essential nature of the whole. (Hegel, *Lectures On Aesthetics*, I, 433.) Because the self-conception of rational agency comprising the content involves its own sensuous manifestation, just as the shape of rational agency comprising the configuration signifies the reality of that agency's autonomy, each side implicitly contains itself in its unity with the other. Hence, Hegel can further maintain that meaning and configuration are here implicitly identical. (*Ibid.*, 433.)

14. As Hegel points out, the introduction of the body of rational agency as a configuration for classical art presupposes the connection of soul and body, an account of which falls outside of aesthetic inquiry into philosophical psychology. (Hegel, *Lectures On Aesthetics*, I, 434.) Needless to say, philosophical psychology, to the extent that it provides the systematic concept of rational agency, is presupposed by every aspect of aesthetics, given how aesthetic worth minimally involves reference to rational agency as creator, audience, and theme of artistic beauty.

15. Hegel, *Lectures On Aesthetics*, I, 432.

16. Hegel, *Lectures On Aesthetics*, I, 434.

17. Hegel, *Lectures On Aesthetics*, I, 432.

18. Hegel, *Lectures On Aesthetics*, I, 434.

19. Hegel, *Lectures On Aesthetics*, I, 436.

20. Hegel, *Lectures On Aesthetics*, I, 435.

21. Hegel, *Lectures On Aesthetics*, I, 433–34.

22. Hegel, *Lectures On Aesthetics*, I, 439.

23. Hegel, *Lectures On Aesthetics*, I, 439.

24. Hegel, *Lectures On Aesthetics*, I, 438, 478.

25. Hegel, *Lectures On Aesthetics*, I, 439.

26. Although Danto might object to classical art having any specific configurations, given how the same shape could be used with wry irreverence for avant garde purposes, this indiscernibility of appearance does not preclude that a certain range of appearances are suited for classical construal in a way in which others are not. Given the contingency of the species being of rational agents, no necessary physical requirements can be mandated for classical art. However, whatever be the natural appearances of rational agents in our and other galaxies, these configurations have a suitability for classical construal that the natural appearances of animals do not.

27. Hegel, *Lectures On Aesthetics*, I, 438–39.

28. Hegel, *Lectures On Aesthetics*, I, 440.

29. Hegel, *Lectures On Aesthetics*, I, 441–42.

30. Hegel, *Lectures On Aesthetics*, I, 476.

31. Hegel, *Lectures On Aesthetics*, I, 502–03.

32. Hegel, *Lectures On Aesthetics*, I, 502.

33. Hegel, *Lectures On Aesthetics*, I, 503.

34. Hegel, *Lectures On Aesthetics*, I, 579.

35. For an extended discussion of the distinction of the moral and the ethical domains of conduct, see Richard Dien Winfield, ***Overcoming Foundations: Studies In Systematic Philosophy*** (New York: Columbia University Press, 1989), Chapter 8, and Richard Dien Winfield, ***Freedom and Modernity*** (Albany: State University of New York Press, 1992), Chapter 6.

36. Drawing upon Hegel's discussion of the epic as a form of classical literature, Georg Lukács makes important arguments to this effect in his *The Theory of The Novel*, trans. by Anna Bostock (Cambridge: MIT Press, 1971).

37. In *The Theory of the Novel*, Lukács uses these terms to describe the integrated civilization comprising the age of the epic. In so doing, Lukács borrows the core of Hegel's account of the world view specific to the classical artform. See Lukács, *The Theory of the Novel*, 29–39.

38. Hegel, *Lectures On Aesthetics*, I, 479.

39. Hegel, *Lectures On Aesthetics*, I, 438.

40. Hegel, *Lectures On Aesthetics*, I, 439.

41. For a detailed argument to support this thesis, see Richard Dien Winfield, *Reason and Justice* (Albany: State University of New York: 1988), Part IV.

42. For arguments supporting this claim, see Richard Dien Winfield, *Overcoming Foundations: Studies In Systematic Philosophy*, Chapter 8, and Richard Dien Winfield, *Freedom and Modernity* (Albany: State University of New York Press, 1992), Chapter 6.

43. Hegel, *Lectures On Aesthetics*, I, 504.

44. Hegel, *Lectures On Aesthetics*, I, 504.

45. Hegel, *Lectures On Aesthetics*, I, 504, 520–21.

46. Hegel, *Lectures On Aesthetics*, I, 504, 520–21.

47. Hegel cites this repose primarily in reference to ancient Greek sculpture, suggesting that it is a characterization of classical visual art, having as its complement, the sightless gaze veiling all clue of an inner self-awareness. (See Hegel, *Lectures On Aesthetics*, I, 520–21.) If that were the case, it would have to be treated within the conception of artistic genres, where the specific realizations of artistic styles in individual arts can first be systematically developed. To sustain the feature of repose as something ingredient in classical art in general, some way would have to be found to make it applicable to non-visual arts, as well as to non-static visual arts, such as theater, film, and dance, and to a static visual art, such as architecture. For this reason, the feature of repose is here introduced in passing.

48. To the degree that Hegel highlights these shortcomings of classical art, he can hardly be charged with embracing a classicism resting upon a doctrine of dialectic as critique of the particularity of the world of civil society, as Peter Szondi maintains. (Peter Szondi, *Poetik und Geschichtsphilosophie I*, 405.) Since civil society is a sphere of self-determination, wherein the pursuit of self-selected particular ends becomes a matter of right, it enjoys a normative validity, provided it does not overwhelm the other spheres of right. Since, as Hegel himself argues in the *Philosophy of Right*, the just state is so organized as to maintain civil society and keep it in its due subordinate place, any conflict between the classical ideal and the pursuits of civil society represents a further mark against the cognitive perfection of classicism.

49. On either account, Hegel's anticipation of a passage beyond classicism to a further artform belies Hegel's reputed embrace of the classical, according to which the demise of classical art should signal the demise of art in general. Although, as we have seen, Hegel does single out the heroic world condition as a backdrop more conducive to artistic construal than the settled order of modern civil society, this does not mean, as Peter Szondi suggests, that the dissolution of

classical art deprives culture of the setting required for artistic configuration. (Peter Szondi, *Poetik und Geschichtsphilosophie I*, 412.) The field of moral engagement will still be available to art under the most prosaic world conditions.

50. Hegel, *Lectures On Aesthetics*, I, 505–06.

51. Hegel, *Lectures On Aesthetics*, I, 506.

52. Hegel, *Lectures On Aesthetics*, I, 509 ff.

53. Hegel, *Lectures On Aesthetics*, I, 510.

54. Hegel, *Lectures On Aesthetics*, I, 511.

55. Hegel, *Lectures On Aesthetics*, I, 511–13.

56. Hegel, *Lectures On Aesthetics*, I, 511.

57. Hegel, *Lectures On Aesthetics*, I, 512.

58. Hegel, *Lectures On Aesthetics*, I, 513.

59. Hegel, *Lectures On Aesthetics*, I, 513.

60. Hegel, *Lectures On Aesthetics*, I, 514. By the same token, Hegel claims that true art is antithetical to the corresponding political world organized around sacrificing individuality on the altar of obedience to abstract laws, a world he sees historically exemplified by ancient Rome, whose own arts consist in the aesthetically questionable genres of comic farce, didactic poetry and satire. (*Ibid.*, I, 514.)

61. Hegel, *Lectures On Aesthetics*, I, 515.

62. Hegel, *Lectures On Aesthetics*, I, 516.

63. Hegel, *Lectures On Aesthetics*, I, 516. Peter Szondi ignores Hegel's recognition of how romanticism can address a particularity of individual agents that, far from setting them at odds with an alien world, unites them with other individuals in civil institutions that foster their right to interact in terms of self-selected aims. (See Szondi, *Poetik und Geschichtsphilosophie I*, 414.)

64. Hegel, *Lectures On Aesthetics*, I, 516.

Chapter 4

1. For a detailed unmasking of the limits of post-modernism, see William Maker, *Philosophy Without Foundations* (Albany: State University of New York Press, 1994), 179–98.

2. Hegel, *Lectures On Aesthetics*, I, 517.

3. This tie to a sensuously given factor is exhibited in how the polis still limits the participation of its members according to their gender and birth, even while supplanting the hegemony of kinship and sacred tradition by a concern for justice as the end of political association.

4. Hegel, *Lectures On Aesthetics*, I, 524.

5. Although Christianity may express this respect in the narrative of Christ, where the divine exists in an actual historical individual, Hegel's suggestion that religious representation must adopt such a narrative in order to uphold the significance of autonomous individual agency is far from evident.

6. However, Hegel does include within romanticism all art of the Christian era, which, he maintains, from its outset begins the progressive working out of a free spirituality liberated from nature, whose full sacred and secular consequences will only be achieved in modern times.

7. Hegel, *Lectures On Aesthetics*, I, 518.

8. Hegel, *Lectures On Aesthetics*, I, 518.

9. Hegel, *Lectures On Aesthetics*, I, 518–19.

10. Hegel, *Lectures On Aesthetics*, I, 519.

11. In just this way, conscience only functions in respect to acting towards other moral selves, whose perceived actuality plays a constitutive role in the choice of moral motives. See "The Limits of Morality" in Winfield, *Overcoming Foundations*, 135–70, and "Morality Without Community" in Winfield, *Freedom and Modernity*, 64–70.

12. Hegel, *Lectures On Aesthetics*, I, 522.

13. Hegel, *Lectures On Aesthetics*, I, 528.

14. Hegel, *Lectures On Aesthetics*, I, 528.

15. Hegel, *Lectures On Aesthetics*, I, 525.

16. Hegel, *Lectures On Aesthetics*, I, 522.

17. Hegel, *Lectures On Aesthetics*, I, 523.

18. See Szondi for an apt analysis of how Hegel presents love as the paradigmatic form of romantic beauty in religious representation. Szondi, *Poetik und Geschichtsphilosophie I*, 445–46.

19. Hegel, *Lectures On Aesthetics*, I, 524.

20. Hegel, *Lectures On Aesthetics*, I, 526–27.

21. Hegel, *Lectures On Aesthetics*, I, 589.

22. Hegel, *Lectures On Aesthetics*, I, 527.

23. Hegel emphasizes how romantic art takes its content from the externally developed doctrine of Christian religion. (Hegel, *Lectures On Aesthetics*, I, 526.) Although this may be historically the case for European Medieval art in particular, it is hardly a necessity for romantic art in general. Not only is Christianity just one conceivable example of a religion fit for romantic construal, but romantic art is free to draw its material from purely secular affairs of the most wide variety.

24. Hegel, *Lectures On Aesthetics*, I, 590.

25. When Lukács describes the novel as "the representative artform of our age" whose "structural categories...constitutively coincide with the world as it is today" (*The Theory of the Novel*, 93.), he seems to depict modernity as an epoch in which interiority stands in an insurmountable opposition to public life. In this respect, his employment of romanticism would seem to be limited to conditions of revolutionary challenge, where traditional ethical community has lost legitimacy without being fully supplanted by institutions of freedom. The novel, however, might still live on under conditions of settled institutions of justice where, because public life no longer contradicts the claims of personal interest and moral autonomy, individual conduct must retreat to the trials of personal conscience to exhibit any exemplary character.

26. Hegel, *Lectures On Aesthetics*, I, 528.

27. As Hegel suggests, the Crusades provide a paradigmatic adventure of chivalry insofar as its participants banded together voluntarily as individuals in pursuit of an end whose debasement of something spiritual into a physical possession left no prize of any worth but the winning of personal honor. (See Hegel, *Lectures On Aesthetics*, I, 587–88.)

28. Szondi, *Poetik und Geschichtsphilosophie I*, 448–49.

29. Hegel, *Lectures On Aesthetics*, I, 590.

30. Hegel, *Lectures On Aesthetics*, I, 590–91.

31. Hegel, *Lectures On Aesthetics*, I, 593.

32. Hegel, *Lectures On Aesthetics*, I, 593.

33. Hegel, *Lectures On Aesthetics*, I, 591.

34. For a discussion of how civil society and democratic government provide institutions of ethical community in conformity with moral subjectivity, see Winfield, *Freedom and Modernity*, 70–71.

35. Hegel discusses such a possibility in his treatment of romantic fiction. See Hegel, *Lectures On Aesthetics*, I, 592–93.

36. Hegel, *Lectures On Aesthetics*, I, 575.

37. To the degree that pathos is generic to character that is artistically construable, the lack of pathos in the agency depicted in this third form of romanticism renders it problematic for art.

38. Hegel, *Lectures On Aesthetics*, I, 577.

39. Hegel characterizes these two alternative configurations of the formal independence of character as "formal firmness of character" and "character as inner but undeveloped totality," respectively. See Hegel, *Lectures On Aesthetics*, I, 577–84.

40. In *The Theory of The Novel*, Lukács applies these dual options in differentiating the two fundamental forms of the novel, the novel of abstract idealism and the novel of disillusionment. See Georg Lukács, *The Theory of The Novel*, trans. by Anna Bostock (Cambridge: The MIT Press, 1971), 97–111, 112–31.

41. Hegel, *Lectures On Aesthetics*, I, 577–80.

42. Hegel, *Lectures On Aesthetics*, I, 579–80.

43. In just this respect, Lukács connects the biographical form of the novel to its treatment of the interconnected predicament of a problematic individual and a contingent world (*The Theory of the Novel*, 78.).

44. Hegel, *Lectures On Aesthetics*, I, 580.

45. Hegel, *Lectures On Aesthetics*, I, 581.

46. Hegel, *Lectures On Aesthetics*, I, 580.

47. Hegel, *Lectures On Aesthetics*, I, 583, 585.

48. For an account of how monological willing is endemically formal, see Winfield, *Reason and Justice*, 160–66, and Winfield, *Freedom and Modernity*, 89–106.

49. For a discussion of how morality is constituted within a structure of interaction that can operate in conjunction with institutions of ethical community, see Winfield, *Overcoming Foundations*, Chapter 8, and Winfield, *Freedom and Modernity*, Chapter 6.

50. Hegel, *Lectures On Aesthetics*, I, 575.

51. Hegel, *Lectures On Aesthetics*, I, 586.

52. Hegel, *Lectures On Aesthetics*, I, 587. Significantly, Hegel maintains that this type of adventure is not just characteristic of the third form of romantic art, but fundamental for romantic construal in general. See Hegel, *Lectures On Aesthetics*, I, 587.

53. Hegel, *Lectures On Aesthetics*, I, 590.

54. Hegel, *Lectures On Aesthetics*, I, 573 ff.

55. These alternatives underlie both Lukács' account of the two forms of the novel: that of abstract idealism and that of disillusionment (The *Theory of the Novel*, 97–131.), and Szondi's analysis of the crisis in modern drama and the "rescue attempts" and "tentative solutions" that seek to resolve the tension between dramatic form and epic content (*The Theory of the Modern Drama*, 11 ff.).

56. Hegel, *Lectures On Aesthetics*, I, 573–74, 595–600, 600–02. He does, however, describe these as aspects of the dissolution of romantic art. (*Ibid.*, 595.)

57. Hegel, *Lectures On Aesthetics*, I, 595–96.

58. Hegel, *Lectures On Aesthetics*, I, 596.

59. Hegel, *Lectures On Aesthetics*, I, 596.

60. Hegel characterizes early modern Dutch art in these terms. See Hegel, *Lectures On Aesthetics*, I, 597–98.

61. This explicit relativization of the content of the image, of course, has its polemical dimension, calling into question accepted norms that may value certain objective forms. For example, Duchamp's found art and Warhol's Brillo boxes both strike at the aesthetic pretensions of the art world and its institutions. However, they do not thereby hark back to the self-understandings of humanity underlying symbolic and classical art, but affirm the independent significance of their own selectivity.

62. Hegel, *Lectures On Aesthetics*, I, 601–602.

63. Similarly, Lukács points out how the irony of the novel does not follow the route of satire and reduce objectivity to a mere plaything of subjectivity. The romantic irony of the novel rather casts its gaze upon the subject itself (including the subject of the authorial voice) to reveal its interconnection to the contingent world opposed to interiority. See, *The Theory of the Novel*, 74–76.

64. Hegel, *Lectures On Aesthetics*, I, 601.

65. This might seem to be the one case where Kant's account of aesthetic judgment might appear to be applicable. However, even here a cognitive element must be paid heed, for unless the audience comprehends that the work's appearance is to be understood as an affirmation of the independent subjectivity from which it originates and to which it is manifest, art succumbs to blind sensation.

66. Since the determination of artforms occurs independently of that of the individual arts, non-objective art cannot here signify simply a form of visual art. It must rather apply to all individual arts, provided that they have the resources for bringing to expression a retreat from the external world and reconstitution of a purely subjective domain of appearance.

67. Although Hegel does not explicitly address abstract art, the latter can easily be characterized in terms of his treatment of the romantic subjective mastery of content, as has been done here. See Hegel, *Lectures On Aesthetics*, I, 599–600.

68. As Charles Taylor points out, when Derrida annihilates all fixed distinctions within the cauldron of deconstruction, nothing is left but the "prodigious power of subjectivity to undo all potential allegiances which might bind it." Charles Taylor, *Sources of The Self: The Making of The Modern Identity* (Cambridge: Harvard University Press, 1989), 489.

69. Charles Taylor describes in these terms how the modernist sensibility remains just as caught up with inwardness as the romantic sensibility from which it distances itself. See Charles Taylor, *Sources of The Self: The Making of The Modern Identity*, 481.

70. Because such "formal independence of individual particularities" can be seen in all the above cases, Szondi is wrong to identify this third stage in Hegel's account of romanticism as nothing but realism. (See Szondi, *Poetik und Geschichtsphilosophie I*, 440.) It does encompass realism, but equally abstract expressionism, serialism, and other varieties of art in which inwardness exhibits its independent mastery over external configurations.

71. Peter Szondi discusses the significance of this connection for the development of art since Hegel's time. See Szondi, *Poetik und Geschichtsphilosophie I*, 438–40.

72. Hegel's account falls short by failing to take into account non-objective art.

73. Peter Szondi objects that Hegel's account of romantic art leaves out a fourth variety, which Szondi identifies as "modern" art, a variety of which Hegel could have no knowledge since it allegedly comprises the type of art that continued to be produced in the century and a half since Hegel's death. (Szondi, *Poetik und Geschichtsphilosophie I*, 461–62.) However, as Szondi himself ends up suggesting, (*Ibid.*, 464–65.) none of the "post-Hegelian" artistic movements to which he refers as exemplars of this fourth type fall beyond the polar extremes of realism and non-objectivism defining the boundaries generic to the third form of romantic art. Further, since these forms are conceptually distinguished, their applicability is not historically relative in the way in which empirically derived models would be.

74. Hegel, *Lectures On Aesthetics*, I, 606.

75. Hegel, *Lectures On Aesthetics*, I, 607.

76. Arthur C. Danto, *The Transfiguration of the Commonplace*, vii, 56.

77. Hegel, *Lectures On Aesthetics*, I, 607, 609.

78. The problem is not that Hegel's unconditioned claims about historical necessity are undermined by the alleged fact that he, like all purveyors of a philosophy of history, are bound to the standpoint of their own age, so that his conception of historical development turns into a self-understanding of one age through the appropriation of past eras. Such an argument, advanced in relation to Hegel's *Lectures On Aesthetics* by Peter Szondi (see Szondi, *Poetik und*

Geschichtsphilosophie I, 433.) is undermined by its own unconditioned global claims about the historicity of any philosophy of history.

79. Hegel, *Lectures On Aesthetics*, I, 594.

80. Hegel, *Lectures On Aesthetics*, I, 594.

81. Hegel, *Lectures On Aesthetics*, I, 528–29.

82. Hegel, *Lectures On Aesthetics*, I, 575.

83. Hegel, *Lectures On Aesthetics*, I, 576, 595.

84. Hegel, *Lectures On Aesthetics*, I, 576, 595, 602.

85. Hegel, *Lectures On Aesthetics*, I, 575.

86. Hegel, *Lectures On Aesthetics*, I 596.

87. Hegel, *Lectures On Aesthetics*, I, 602.

CHAPTER 5

1. Arthur C. Danto, *The Transfiguration of The Commonplace: A Philosophy of Art* (Cambridge: Harvard University Press, 1981), 138.

2. It was this possibility that allowed the question to arise as to whether the artforms should be conceived before, after, or coevally with the individual arts. If, however, the individuation of genres is predicated upon the differentiation of artforms, then the system of arts must be conceived after the artforms.

3. Hegel, *Lectures On Aesthetics*, I, 613–14.

4. Stephen Bungay, *Beauty and Truth: A Study of Hegel's Aesthetics*, 91–92.

5. Stephen Bungay wrongly claims this exclusive a priori character for a spatio-temporal division, (Bungay, *Beauty and Truth*, 91.) ignoring first, how the modes of sensibility may be susceptible of an a priori determination, secondly, how the varieties of sensible existence corresponding to those modes could be a priori, and thirdly, how the concept of art limits those senses and varieties of existence that are susceptible of entering into aesthetic experience.

6. That individuals of a species of rational agents lack certain senses no more precludes arts employing media directed at those senses than does the possibility of an entire species of rational agents being blind, deaf, numb, or deprived of taste or smell. Although such arts cannot be appreciated by audiences consisting in those individuals, an account of the system of arts must address the possible modes of sensory perception, however they be distributed.

7. As binary digital systems exhibit, a language can be expressed in any medium allowing of two contrasting factors, susceptible of combination and

alternation. Hence, as long as at least two different tastes or smells are recognizable and reproducible, taste and smell can conceivably be used to communicate literature.

8. Immanuel Kant, *Critique of Judgment*, trans. by Werner S. Pluhar (Indianapolis: Hackett, 1987), footnote 58, p. 190 (Ak. V, 320).

9. Kant, *Critique of Judgment*, 190 (Ak. V, 321).

10. Kant, *Critique of Judgment*, 190–94 (Ak. V, 321–24).

11. Kant, *Critique of Judgment*, 190–94 (Ak. V, 321–24).

12. Kant, *Critique of Judgment*, 190 (Ak. V, 321).

13. Schelling quite rightly objects that Kant's characterization of music as a play of feelings, as if its purpose were the awakening of emotions, is too formal to distinguish music from conglomerations of smell, tastes, or other sensations devoid of aesthetic significance. See F. W. J. Schelling, *The Philosophy of Art*, trans. by Douglas W. Stott (Minneapolis: University of Minnesota Press, 1989), 103.

14. Hegel, *Lectures On Aesthetics*, I, 622.

15. Hegel, *Lectures On Aesthetics*, I, 623.

16. Hegel, *Lectures On Aesthetics*, I, 623.

17. Arthur C. Danto, *The Transfiguration of The Commonplace*, 136.

18. Consequently, even if the physical being of an artwork does not unequivocally identify its genre, the nature of each genre dictates what kind of thing can figure within it as well as what meaning can inform a particular art object within its domain. In this respect, it makes little sense for Danto to acknowledge that the experiments of artists "are defined by the rules of the genre they are working in" and yet dismiss a theory of genres as an exercise in pedantry. (Arthur C. Danto, *The Transfiguration of The Commonplace*, 138.)

19. Charles Karelis points out this conformity in his interpretative introduction to Hegel's *Introduction To Aesthetics*, trans. by T. M. Knox (Oxford: Oxford University Press, 1979), lx.

20. Hegel, *Lectures On Aesthetics*, I, 614.

21. Hegel, *Lectures On Aesthetics*, I, 624.

22. Kant, *Critique of Judgment*, 191 (Ak. V, 322).

23. That a building could represent an independently existing thing, as a fast-food restaurant might resemble a giant hamburger, could be considered incidental to its architectural character.

24. Yet, significantly, the mere externality of architectural configuration does not tie it to a *particular* content. Any world view that achieves expression in architecture will manifest its content in the organization of heavy material.

25. Hegel, *Lectures On Aesthetics*, I, 624–25.

26. Hegel, *Lectures On Aesthetics*, I, 625.

27. Bungay, *Beauty and Truth*, 94.

28. Hegel, *Lectures On Aesthetics*, I, 625.

29. Bungay erroneously claims that Hegel's description of literature is incompatible with the divisions by artforms because Hegel characterizes literature as corresponding to all three artforms in equal measure. (See Bungay, *Art and Beauty*, 90.) Although Hegel does differentiate the genres of epic, lyric, and dramatic poetry by harking back to the artforms, this internal division of literature need not preclude literature as a whole from exhibiting a romantic character. Other difficulties undermine this alleged affinity between literature and the romantic style.

30. As Bungay points out, although music may have a greater "interiority" than painting, it is far from clear that this translates into an "increasing spiritual content," availing more access to the depths of inner subjectivity. (Bungay, *Beauty and Truth*, 93.) Although music adds a temporal dimension, permitting a display of changing moods whereby character reveals itself in the process of its transformations, painting, though limited to a single image conveying one moment in the life of rational agency, adds the discursive dimension of pictorial representation, allowing for a far richer portrayal of the situation in which action proceeds.

31. This capability applies specifically to representational, as opposed to abstract painting. Hegel takes for granted that painting is representational, just as he takes for granted that sculpture represents the human figure.

32. Hegel, *Lectures On Aesthetics*, I, 626.

33. Hegel himself identifies this final art as that of poetry. However, as Charles Karelis observes, what Hegel discusses under the rubric of poetry roughly falls under the common heading of literature, with the exclusion of such "prosaic" literary works as histories and orations. (Charles Karelis, "An Interpretative Essay" in Hegel's *Introduction To Aesthetics*, lxxi.) To the degree that the latter, despite their literary merit, are essentially prosaic in character, it makes sense to identify Hegel's final art as the art of literature.

34. Hegel, *Lectures On Aesthetics*, I, 626–27.

35. As Karelis points out, Hegel is somewhat ambiguous regarding this aspect of literature. See Charles Karelis, "An Interpretative Essay" in Hegel's *Introduction To Aesthetics*, lxxii.

36. Hegel, *Lectures On Aesthetics*, I, 626.

37. Hegel, *Lectures On Aesthetics*, I, 626.

38. As Stephen Bungay observes, the fact that the division by artforms leaves painting and music indistinguishable (and he should have also added, liter-

ature) is sufficient of itself to disqualify the artforms as the ultimate principle for differentiating the arts. See Bungay, *Beauty and Truth*, 90.

39. Hegel, *Lectures On Aesthetics*, I, 628.

40. The problem plaguing Hegel's account is not, as Bungay wrongly insists, that Hegel conflates history and systematics. (Bungay, *Beauty and Truth*, 90, 102.) The artforms are not, properly speaking, historical categories, but rather determinations of the possible forms of artistic construal. The problem rather lies in that the artforms, being ***particular*** modes common in principle to each individual genre, cannot serve to individuate the arts. Vittorio Hösle is more on target when he criticizes Hegel's differentiation of the arts in terms of the artforms for neglecting how individual arts are pursued in epochs of different styles and for suggesting that painting has more in common with music and poetry than with other visual arts. However, Hösle's proposed remedy, employing the poetic genres of epic, lyric, and drama, as organizing principles for differentiating the arts, succumbs to the same basic logical incoherence by using factors common to a single art (literature) to individuate the different arts. Hösle's recasting of the epic-lyric-drama trichotomy as a triad of objectivity-subjectivity-intersubjectivity is of no avail, since it employs terms that are extraneous to the individuating factors of the arts, as evident in how individual arts can each exhibit objective, subjective and intersubjective dimensions alike. See Vittorio *Hösle, Hegels System—Band 2: Philosophie der Nature und des Geistes* (Hamburg: Meine Verlag, 1988), 636–37.

41. This is the conclusion that Bungay all too precipitously draws from the collapse of Hegel's division by artform. See Bungay, *Beauty and Truth*, 90, 91.

Index

abstract art, see non-representational art
abstract expressionism, 91, 92, 132 n. 70
Adorno, Theodor W., 1
aesthetic judgment, 3; see also aesthetic reception
aesthetic reception, 3, 5, 112; of classical art, 66, 93; of romantic art, 93; of symbolic art, 38, 93
aesthetic value, see beauty
aesthetics, 1, 7, 8; as the philosophy of art, 4; metaphysical 2, 3, 4, 115 n. 4; systematic 99, 113, 118 n. 23; transcendental 2–3, 4, 115 n. 5
aleatory art, 55
allegory, 46, 47, 120 n. 15
architecture, 105, 107, 108–10, 113, 134 nn. 23, 24
Aristophanes, 69
Aristotle, 2, 56
art: individuality of, 4; of the sublime, see symbolic art; origin of, 38–40; originality of, 3
art appreciation, see art criticism
art criticism, 2, 3, 8, 10; see also aesthetic reception
art history, 3, 5, 9, 10, 13, 36, 41, 67–68, 76–77, 79, 80, 94, 99, 101, 117 n. 13, 122 n. 53
art world, 3, 131 n. 61
artforms, 1, 3, 5, 7; hierarchy of, 19–21; as historical cultural unities, 17–19; interrelation of, 28, 94; logical differentiation of, 15–17, 21–22, 74–75, 117 n. 11; as particularizations of art, 14–15; relation to individual arts, 8–13, 15; see also symbolic, classical and romantic art
artifact, 4, 32
artist, anonymity of in symbolic creation, 38
artistic beauty, see beauty
artistic creation, 3, 4–5; of classical art, 65–66; of romantic art, 92–93; of symbolic art, 37–38; role of technique in, 3
artistic style, see style
artwork, 1, 3

beauty, 3; as self-understanding, 4, 5, 13; individuality of, 3, 15, 16
Benjamin, Walter, 1

Bungay, Stephen, 9–11, 16, 102, 133 n. 5, 135 nn. 29, 30, 38, 136 nn. 40, 41

Carter, Curtis L., 118 n. 25
categorial immanence, 26, 33, 41, 52, 69
character: artistic representation of, 37, 111; formal independence of, 79, 86–88, 94, 95, 97, 130 nn. 37, 39, 40
chivalry, as an object of artistic construal, 79, 82–83, 84, 85, 93, 94, 95, 97, 129 n. 27
Christianity, 80, 128 nn. 5, 6, 129 n. 23
civil society, as an object of artistic construal, 76, 85, 126 n. 48
classical art, 2, 19, 20, 23–24, 25, 39, 51–71, 75, 90, 92, 95, 110, 111, 112, 119 n. 35, 126 n. 48; and Greek art, 17, 110, 112; and truth, 66–67; as employing the shape of rational agency, 57–59, 81, 125 n. 26; as giving art central cultural importance, 20, 21; as most beautiful artform, 19, 52; as privileging sculpture, 108–09; construal of conduct, 64, 66–67, 128 n. 3; construal of the divine, 63–64, 67, 79; dissolution of, 66–71, 96; relation to symbolic art, 40–41, 48, 49, 51–52, 53–57, 59, 61–62
comedy, 83, 85, 89
comparative art, see symbolic art
conduct, 4; as an object of artistic beauty, 36–37; precipitating situation of 37, 81; world condition of, 36–37, 78–79, 82
conscience, see morality
culinary art, 103

dada, 92
dance, 102, 111, 113
Danto, Arthur C., 93, 100, 106, 124 n. 12, 125 n. 26, 134 n. 18
death, as an object of artistic construal, 80; of art, see end of art
deconstruction, 132 n. 68
Derrida, Jacques, 132 n. 68
descriptive poetry, 47–48, 71, 95
didactic poetry, 47–48, 71, 95, 123 n. 66
divine, as a content of artistic construal, 34–36
drama, 102, 118 n. 23, 131 n. 55, 135 n. 29
Duchamp, Marcel, 131 n. 61

end of art, 19–21, 93–97, 117 n. 10, 118 n. 25, 126 n. 49
epic, 2, 64, 125 nn. 36, 37, 131 n. 55, 135 n. 29
epigram, 48

film, 101, 102, 113
"found" art, 55, 90
freedom, see also self-determination

Gadamer, Hans-Georg, 116, n. 6
gardening, as art, 111
genre, 2; see also individual arts
Gothic architecture, 110
graphic arts, 104
Greek art, 17, 59–60, 62, 110, 112

Hegel, Georg Wilhelm Friedrich, 1, 5, 8, 9, 10, 14, 16, 19, 20, 120 n. 15; *Lectures on Aesthetics,* 5, 53; on classical art, 19, 20, 21, 23–24, 25, 39, 51–56, 59–64, 66–71, 103, 123 n. 66, 124 nn. 13, 14, 125 nn. 36, 37, 126 n. 47, 48, 49; on Roman art, 127 n. 60; on romantic art, 19, 24–25, 26, 68, 76–80, 82, 87, 89–92, 94–97, 128 nn. 5, 6, 129 nn. 23, 27, 35, 130 n. 52, 131 nn. 56, 60, 67, 132 nn. 72, 73, 135 n. 29; on

satire, 69–71, 127 n. 60; on symbolic art, 22–23, 24, 25, 27–32, 35–36, 38–49, 121 nn. 42, 45, 47, 53, 123 n. 63; on the differentiation of artforms, 22, 26, 117 n. 14; on the differentiation of individual arts, 106–12, 113, 135 nn. 29, 31, 33, 35; on the end of art, 19, 76–77, 94–97
Heidegger, Martin, 118 n. 21
heroic age, see world condition, of revolutionary challenge
holography, 101, 113
Hösle, Vittorio, 25, 136 n. 40
humanity, see also rational agency
Hume, David, 2

immanent categorial development, see categorial immanence
impressionism, 90
individual arts, 1, 7, 64, 99–113; as differentiated by analogy to speech, 104–06; as differentiated by appeal to the artforms, 106–12, 135–36 n. 38, 136 n. 41; as differentiated by media, 15, 101–04; logic of their differentiation, 99–101, 133 nn. 5, 6, 134 n. 18; relation to artforms, 8–13, 33, 100–01, 113, 133, n. 2, 136 n. 40; see also architecture, dance, drama, graphic arts, literature, music, painting, performing arts, plastic arts, sculpture, visual arts
individuality: logic of, 8, 10; of art, 3, 11, 15, 16, 32
interpretation, 8
irony, 91, 131 n. 63

Kant, Immanuel, 2–3, 103, 105, 108, 112, 116 n. 6, 131 n. 65, 134 n. 13
Karelis, Charles, 134 n. 19, 135 nn. 33, 35

language, in art, 101, 104, 133 n. 7; see also literature
literature, 2, 102, 104, 105, 106, 107, 110–112, 113, 134 n. 7, 135 nn. 33, 35
Lukács, Georg, 1, 64, 125 nn. 36, 37, 129 n. 25, 130 nn. 40, 43, 131 nn. 55, 63
lyric poetry, 2, 135 n. 29

Maker, William, 127 n. 1
Mao Zedong, 2
Marxist aesthetics, 14
meaning and configuration: modes of their unity in art, 15–17, 21–22; unity of in art, 4, 9, 12, 13, 29
medium, artistic, 1, 2, 8, 9, 10, 11, 12, 13, 14–15, 101–04
metaphysical aesthetics, see aesthetics, metaphysical
mimesis, 34, 35, 46, 60, 90
minimalism, 55, 112
modernity, 2, 17, 19, 73–74, 79, 82, 88, 126 n. 49, 129 n. 25
morality, as an object of artistic construal, 58, 64, 67, 76, 81–82, 84, 85, 86, 88, 109, 111, 127 n. 49, 128 n. 11, 129 n. 25, 130 n. 49
music, 2, 102, 104, 105, 106, 107, 110–112, 113, 134 n. 13, 135 n. 30

naive and sentimental art, 17; see also Schiller
naturalism, 90
Nietzsche, Friedrich, 1
non-representational art, 34–35, 91, 105, 108, 112, 131 nn. 66, 67, 132 nn. 72, 73, 135 n. 31; see also abstract expressionism
novel, 64, 129 nn. 25, 35, 130 nn. 40, 43, 131 nn. 55, 63

opera, 111
Oriental art, 17, 36; see also symbolic art

painting, 105, 107, 110–112, 113, 122 n. 50, 135 nn. 30, 31
pathos, as an object of artistic construal, 64, 83, 86, 87, 130 n. 37
perfume, as art, 103
philosophy: of mind, 103, 124 n. 14; of nature, 101
photorealism, 90
photography, 101
plastic arts, 102, 104, 108, 110
Plato, 2, 60
poetry, 105, 122 n. 50
pop-art, 90
post-heroic world condition, see world condition, of established institutions of justice
postmodernism, 73–74, 90–92, 118 n. 21, 127 n. 1

rational agency, 57, 118 n. 26; as the privileged shape in classical art, 57–59, 81, 109
realism, 90, 92, 132 nn. 70, 73
religion, 4
Renaissance, 25, 79
rhetoric, 105
romantic art, 2, 16, 19, 20, 24–25, 26, 39, 55, 68, 71, 73–97, 109–10, 117 n. 10, 119 n. 35, 132 nn. 69, 73; and freedom, 75–76, 77–78, 81–82, 85, 92–93; and modernity, 17, 19–20, 73–74, 82, 84–86, 97, 129 n. 25; as most truthful artform, 19, 20, 95; as privileging painting, music and literature, 110–12; as the end of art, 76–77, 93–97; character, formal independence of, 79, 86–88, 94, 95, 97, 130 nn. 37, 39, 40; construal of conduct, 76, 80–89; construal of the divine, 76, 79–80, 128 n. 18; options in a post-revolutionary world, 84–86, 127 n. 63, 129 n. 25; options in a world of revolutionary challenge, 82–84, 129 n. 25; relation to classical art, 68–69, 94
romanticism, see romantic art
Rorty, Richard, 118 n. 21
Rose, Gillian, 117 n. 10, 118 nn. 27, 28, 119 n. 35
Rosen, Charles, 1

satire, 69, 70–71, 91, 95, 96, 131 n. 63
Schelling, F. W. J., 1, 17, 103, 117 n. 16, 134 n. 13
Schiller, Friedrich, 1, 17; on naive and sentimental art, 17, 117 n. 16
Schlegel, Friedrich, 1
science, 4
sculpture, 105, 107, 108–10, 112, 113, 122 n. 50, 126 n. 47
self-determination: and normative validity, 66, 73–74, 120 n. 34; and the concrete universal, 54; in art, 4, 66–67, 74; logic of, 56, 88
senses, in relation to art, 103–104
serialism, 132 n. 70
Shakespeare, W., 117 n. 16
Shapiro, Meyer, 116 n. 7, 117 n. 13
sign, 29, 30, 31, 92
style, 1, 2, 5, 10; and the individual artist, 18; as a cultural unity, 17–18; formal taxonomies of, 13–14; see also art forms
sublime, the: 23, 35, 44, 121 n. 47; and symbolic art, 23, 37, 43–45, 46, 49, 54, 79, 121 n. 47, 122 n. 50
surrealism, 92
symbol, 29–31, 120 n. 15
symbolic art, 16, 20, 22–23, 24, 25, 27–49, 57, 65, 66, 75, 92, 95, 109, 111, 112, 118 n. 28, 121 n. 47; and oriental art, 17, 36; as an art of the sublime, 23, 24, 43–45, 46, 49, 54, 66, 122 n. 47; as

comparative art, 45–48, 49, 54, 70, 91, 95, 96, 123 n. 63; construal of conduct in, 36–37; construal of the divine in, 34–36, 79, 121 n. 42; primacy of, 27–29, 31, 38–40, 42; privileged relation to architecture, 108; relation to other artforms, 27–29, 38, 40–41; role of symbol in, 29–33; unconscious symbolism, 42–43, 44, 45, 49, 121 nn. 42, 45, 47; varieties of, 40–49, 123 n. 61
systematic philosophy, 10, 103
Szondi, Peter, 1, 117 n. 11, n. 20, 118 n. 23, 120 n. 26, 122 nn. 50, 61, 126 nn. 48, 49, 127 n. 63, 128 n. 18, 130 n. 55, 132 nn. 70, 71, 73, 78

Taylor, Charles, 132 nn. 68, 69
technique, 32, 46
theater, 113, see also drama
tragedy, 2, 87; see also drama
transcendental philosophy, 3
transfiguration in art, 4
truth, of art, 39

unconscious symbolism, see symbolic art

video, 113
Vischer, Friedrich Theodor, 25
visual arts, 102, 104, 105, 106, 113, 131 n. 66
von Ulrici, 25

Warhol, A., 131 n. 61
Weisse, Ch. H., 25
Wölfflin, Heinrich, 14